# BEYOND ROE

# BEYOND ROE

*Why Abortion Should be Legal—Even if the Fetus is a Person*

David Boonin

# OXFORD
UNIVERSITY PRESS

Oxford University Press is a department of the University of Oxford. It furthers the University's objective of excellence in research, scholarship, and education by publishing worldwide. Oxford is a registered trade mark of Oxford University Press in the UK and certain other countries.

Published in the United States of America by Oxford University Press
198 Madison Avenue, New York, NY 10016, United States of America.

© Oxford University Press 2019

All rights reserved. No part of this publication may be reproduced, stored in a retrieval system, or transmitted, in any form or by any means, without the prior permission in writing of Oxford University Press, or as expressly permitted by law, by license, or under terms agreed with the appropriate reproduction rights organization. Inquiries concerning reproduction outside the scope of the above should be sent to the Rights Department, Oxford University Press, at the address above.

You must not circulate this work in any other form
and you must impose this same condition on any acquirer.

Library of Congress Cataloging-in-Publication Data
Names: Boonin, David, author.
Title: Beyond roe : why abortion should be legal—even if the fetus is a person / David Boonin.
Description: New York : Oxford University Press, [2019] |
Includes bibliographical references and index.
Identifiers: LCCN 2018029351 | ISBN 9780190904845 (pbk.) |
ISBN 9780190904838 (hardback case cover) | ISBN 9780190904852 (updf) |
ISBN 9780190904869 (epub)
Subjects: LCSH: Abortion—Moral and ethical aspects. | Abortion—Law and legislation.
Classification: LCC HQ767.15 .B658 2019 | DDC 179.7/6—dc23
LC record available at https://lccn.loc.gov/2018029351

9 8 7 6 5 4 3 2 1

Paperback Printed by Webcom, Inc., Canada
Hardback Printed by Bridgeport National Bindery, Inc., United States of America

*For Harriet, Leah, and Sadie Boonin*

# Contents

Preface | ix

PART I  Why Abortion Should Be Legal

1. An Unusual Case | 3
2. The Lesson of the Case | 7
3. Changing the Case | 13
4. Hypothetical Cases | 18
5. Contraceptive Failure | 21
6. Failure to Use Contraception | 31
7. Sex Selection | 37
8. Genetic Screening | 41
9. Viability | 45
10. Infanticide | 49
11. Feticide | 52

## PART II  Objections and Responses

12. Consent | 59

13. Responsibility | 69

14. Child Support | 84

15. Parents | 88

16. Children | 96

17. Natural Purposes | 100

18. Cause of Death | 107

19. Intentions | 121

20. Other Differences | 127

21. Other Objections | 135

## PART III  Why Abortion Should Be Less Restricted

22. Insurance Restrictions | 143

23. The Hyde Amendment | 151

24. Mandatory Waiting Periods | 157

25. Mandatory Counseling | 169

26. Mandatory Ultrasounds | 181

27. Parental Consent and Notification | 187

28. Other Restrictions | 195

29. Summary and Conclusion | 199

POSTSCRIPT | 209
INDEX | 211

# Preface

In 1971, the philosopher Judith Jarvis Thomson published an article called "A Defense of Abortion." It has become one of the most widely discussed articles in contemporary philosophy. Two years later, in the case of *Roe v. Wade*, the U.S. Supreme Court produced its own defense of abortion, striking down a variety of legal restrictions on the practice by a vote of 7–2. The majority opinion, written by Justice Harry Blackmun, has become one of the most widely discussed opinions in contemporary law.

Thomson's article and Blackmun's opinion point in the same direction. They both support a woman's right to have an abortion. But in one important respect, Thomson's argument goes beyond Blackmun's. The argument in Blackmun's opinion depends on the claim that "the word 'person,' as used in the Fourteenth Amendment, does not include the unborn." Invoking a right to privacy on the part of the pregnant woman, the majority opinion in *Roe v. Wade* makes the case that abortion should be legal, at least in the first two trimesters, if the fetus is not a person. But the court's decision provides no reason to think abortion should be legal if the fetus is a person. Thomson's article, while focusing on the moral question rather than the legal question, argues that abortion is morally permissible even if the fetus is a person and even if this means the fetus has a right to life. Unlike Blackmun's argument, then, Thomson's argument doesn't depend on rejecting the claim that the fetus is a person.

My main goal in this book is to take the argument that Thomson pioneered in the moral context, adapt it to the legal context, and use it to argue that abortion should be legal even if the fetus is a person. That's one way this book aims to go beyond *Roe*. I present and develop an argument for this claim in part I and respond to objections to the argument in part II. I don't try to show that abortion should be legal through all nine months of pregnancy, though maybe it should be, and I don't insist my argument shows that every method of abortion should be legal, though maybe it does, but I do try to show that even if the fetus is a person, at least some forms of abortion should be legal at least until the fetus is viable. My other goal in this book is to take the kind of analysis that Thomson pioneered and use it to argue that abortion should be much less restricted in this country than it currently is. While the Supreme Court has struck down many abortion restrictions since 1973, it has also held that many others are compatible with its ruling in *Roe v. Wade*. I argue in part III that even if the fetus is a person, many of the abortion restrictions the court has upheld should be abolished. That's the second way this book aims to go beyond *Roe*.

Since the reasoning in *Roe* depends on the claim that the fetus is not a person, and since the claim that the fetus is not a person is highly controversial, my hope is that in going beyond *Roe* in these two ways, this book can help to strengthen the case for abortion rights. If you already think of yourself as pro-choice, I hope the argument of this book will provide a valuable addition to your thinking. If you consider yourself pro-life, I hope you'll at least come to think there's more to the pro-choice position than you might have realized. If you locate yourself somewhere in between, I hope you'll find some help here in working out your thinking on the subject. If you're already familiar with the basic idea behind Thomson's argument, I hope you'll benefit from seeing how it can be applied and developed in some unfamiliar ways. And if you aren't yet familiar with Thomson's argument, I hope you'll find this a useful introduction to a distinctive and important approach to the controversy over abortion.

Finally, and more generally, I hope this book will help to illustrate some of the ways that philosophical thinking can usefully be brought to bear on important matters of public concern. Thomson's article originally appeared in the first issue of a journal whose title, *Philosophy and Public Affairs*, reflected an emerging commitment by a growing number of philosophers to apply the tools of their trade to real-life controversies taking place outside the ivory tower. One thing philosophers are trained to do is provide a careful analysis of the meaning of key terms. At the time that Thomson's article was published, for example, one side of the public debate over abortion claimed that the fetus has a right to life while the other side denied that the fetus has a right to life, but neither side really seemed to stop and ask what, exactly, it means to have a right to life. If a person has a right to life, that is, what specifically does that entitle them to? And, perhaps, more importantly, what does it not entitle them to? Thomson made a crucial contribution to the abortion debate precisely because she stopped to ask that question.

Philosophers are also trained to combine the terms they use into arguments that clearly distinguish between the assumptions they're making and the conclusions they're attempting to derive from them, to subject their assumptions to critical scrutiny by carefully probing them for possible counterexamples, and to test the limits of their positions to avoid claiming more than their reasoning entitles them to claim. When they publish their work in scholarly journals, philosophers often use technical terms and engage extensively with the works of other philosophers who have written on the subject at issue. I've done my best in what follows to use the same philosophical tools they use in the journals but in a more informal and accessible manner.

So if you're a student reading this book for a philosophy class, I hope what follows will encourage you to see the analytical tools the class gives you as something you can apply to the real world outside the classroom. If you're a student reading this book for a class in some other department, I hope it will encourage you to consider taking a philosophy class. And if you've come to this book from outside of academia altogether, I hope it will encourage you to seek out more works by philosophers who are trying to apply their area of expertise to concrete issues that concern you. The application of abstract philosophical reasoning to practical matters of public concern has blossomed in recent years in ways that would have been hard to imagine when Thomson first published her article. I hope this book can contribute to its continued flourishing.

# BEYOND ROE

**PART I**

# WHY ABORTION SHOULD BE LEGAL

# 1

## An Unusual Case

Robert McFall was an asbestos worker from Pittsburgh. In 1978, he was diagnosed with aplastic anemia. The doctors told him he'd die if he didn't get a bone marrow transplant. And they said he needed one soon. Preliminary tests for tissue compatibility were quickly conducted. Only one promising candidate was found: a cousin of McFall's named David Shimp. Before additional tests could confirm his compatibility, though, Shimp had a change of heart. He refused to submit to further testing. And he declared that he wouldn't give McFall any of his bone marrow even if it was needed to save McFall's life. Running out of options at that point, McFall decided to sue Shimp. In the motion filed by his attorney, McFall asked the court to order Shimp to undergo the additional testing and, if the results were positive, to order Shimp to give him the bone marrow he needed. The case of *McFall v. Shimp* was heard in the Common Pleas Court of Allegheny County by Judge John P. Flaherty Jr. in July of that year.

Judge Flaherty wasn't impressed by McFall's petition. While he clearly felt sorry for the man, he just as clearly felt his lawsuit was absurd. For the state to force Shimp to give McFall the bone marrow he needed, the judge wrote in his decision, "would change the very concept and principle upon which our society is founded," a principle, as he put it, of "respect for the individual." In fact, Judge Flaherty went even further than this, adding: "For a society which respects the rights of one individual, to sink its teeth into the jugular vein or neck of one of its members and suck from it sustenance for another member, is revolting to our hard-wrought concepts of jurisprudence." Needless to say, he denied McFall's request for an injunction against Shimp. Judge Flaherty's ruling was issued on July 26, 1978. Fifteen days later, Robert McFall was dead.

Now let's not worry about legal jargon or technicalities. Judge Flaherty's basic point was simple: it would be wrong for the state to force Shimp to give McFall the bone marrow he needed. I'll bet you agree with Judge Flaherty about this. You might disapprove of Shimp's refusal to donate the bone marrow his cousin needed, but you probably think it would have been wrong for the state to force Shimp to donate it once Shimp had decided he wasn't willing to do so. Even McFall's sister agreed that Shimp had the right to decide what to do. So for the purposes of this book, I'm going to assume you agree with the judge on this point. And assuming you do agree, I'm going to try to convince you that abortion should be legal even if you think every fetus is a person and has a right to life.

Now trying to use your belief about McFall and Shimp to support my claim about abortion may initially strike you as implausible, for two reasons. First, while Americans remain sharply divided over abortion, there's one thing both sides of the debate generally seem to believe: that if the fetus is a person, then abortion should be illegal. The standard pro-life position says the fetus is a person and has a right to life, that abortion is therefore murder, and that because abortion is murder the government should prohibit it. The standard pro-choice response doesn't say the government should sometimes permit murder. Instead, it says the fetus isn't really a person and that because the fetus isn't a person, abortion isn't murder in the first place. People who are pro-life and people who are pro-choice disagree about whether abortion should be legal, that is, but they seem largely united in the belief that whether the state should ban abortion depends on whether the fetus is a person. The main goal of this book is to convince you they're wrong about this. Abortion should be legal even if the fetus is a person. So whether you consider yourself pro-life, pro-choice, or somewhere in between, you'll probably start out thinking the claim I'm going to try to convince you of in this book is implausible.

The second reason what I'm going to try to do in this book may initially strike you as implausible has less to do with the claim I'm going to try to defend and more to do with the way I'm going to try to defend it. I've explained the basic facts involved in the case of *McFall v. Shimp*. I've said I'm going to assume you think it would have been wrong for the state to force Shimp to give McFall the bone marrow he needed. And I've said I'm going to try to use this belief of yours to support my claim that abortion should be legal even if the fetus is a person. But it may seem hard to imagine how this approach could possibly work. Neither Robert McFall nor David Shimp were pregnant. Nor, as far as I know, was anyone else involved in the case. Their dispute involved no fetus, no abortion, not even a uterus. So it may seem implausible to think a claim about the judge's ruling in this case could give us a reason to conclude anything about abortion, let alone give us a reason to conclude that abortion should be legal even if the fetus is a person.

I admit that on the face of it, the case of *McFall v. Shimp* has nothing to do with abortion. But I think we can extract a general lesson from the case and then apply that lesson to abortion. Once we see what that general lesson is, and what it commits us to, I think we'll see that abortion should be legal even if the fetus is a person. This conclusion is at odds with the way most people think about abortion and that may make them think the claim I'm going to try to defend in this book is implausible. But once we see what the general lesson of *McFall v. Shimp* is and what it commits us to, I think we'll see that the claim that abortion should be legal even if the fetus is a person is quite plausible. In fact, I think we'll see that it's true.

So for the purposes of this book, I'm also going to assume, at least for the sake of the argument, that every human fetus is a person and that every human fetus has a right to life. In part I, I'm going to try to convince you that even if this assumption is true, abortion should still be legal. In part II, I'll discuss a variety of objections that can be raised against my position and try to convince you not to accept them. In part III, I'll then try to convince you that even if every fetus is a person, abortion should not only be legal but should also be much less restricted than it currently is. And I'll try to convince you of all this by depending only on assumptions I think you'll accept no matter what your current view of abortion is. This approach to trying to resolve the abortion debate may strike you as unusual and that might also make you initially skeptical. But look at it this way: the traditional approach of trying to resolve the debate over whether abortion should be legal by first trying to get everyone to agree about whether the fetus is a person doesn't seem to be working too well. The view I'm going to try to defend in this book offers the possibility of resolving the debate over whether abortion should be legal without having to wait until we've first resolved the debate over whether the fetus is a person. Because this would be such an important result if it could be achieved, it seems to me worth thinking about carefully, even if the chances of success at the outset seem slim. And thinking about this possibility carefully is what this book tries to help you do.

# 2

## The Lesson of the Case

Let's start with the claim that abortion should be legal in cases of rape and work our way to other cases from there. And just to keep things simple, let's start by imagining a case where it's perfectly clear that the woman who wants to have an abortion did nothing to consent to the act of sex that led to her pregnancy. So consider the case of Alice, a 23-year-old software engineer from St. Louis. One day, while Alice was busy working at her desk, a stranger slipped a drug into her coffee that rendered her unconscious. While she was knocked out, this stranger had sex with her. Several weeks later, Alice discovered she was pregnant. She doesn't want to be. One thing I'm trying to convince you of in this book is that it should be legal for Alice to have an abortion in this situation and that this is true even if we assume the fetus developing inside her body is a person with a right to life.

Now what, you may be starting to wonder, does any of this have to do with the case of *McFall v. Shimp*? We can begin to answer this question by first answering a different one: Why are we so confident that it would have been wrong in that case for the state to force Shimp to let McFall use his bone marrow? As far as I can tell, there's only one plausible answer to that question. The state didn't have the right to force Shimp to let McFall use his bone marrow because McFall didn't have the right to use Shimp's bone marrow. If McFall did have the right to use Shimp's bone marrow, after all, it's hard to see what would have been wrong with the state's stepping in to enforce that right. So if you agree that it would have been wrong for the state to force Shimp to let McFall use his bone marrow, you should agree that McFall didn't have the right to use Shimp's bone marrow.

I'm now going to assume you agree that McFall didn't have the right to use Shimp's bone marrow. I'm also going to assume you accept two other claims that weren't in dispute. First, McFall was a person who had a right to life. Second, McFall needed Shimp's bone marrow. So there are now three claims I'm assuming you accept: McFall was a person, McFall needed Shimp's bone marrow, and McFall didn't have the right to Shimp's bone marrow. If you accept these three claims, you're now in a position to draw an important conclusion: being a person doesn't give you the right to use another person's bone marrow even if you need to use it. After all, if being a person did give you the right to use another person's bone marrow if you needed to use it, then McFall would have had the right to use Shimp's bone marrow, since McFall was a person and McFall needed to use Shimp's bone marrow. But McFall didn't have the right to use Shimp's bone marrow even though McFall was a person and he needed to use Shimp's bone marrow. So being a person doesn't give you the right to use another person's bone marrow even if you need to use it.

The same goes for having a right to life. Having a right to life doesn't give you the right to use another person's bone marrow even if you need to use it. If it did, then since McFall had a right to life and needed to use Shimp's bone marrow, he would have had the right to use Shimp's bone marrow. But McFall didn't have the right to use Shimp's bone marrow even though McFall had a right to life and he needed to use Shimp's bone marrow. So having a right to life, like being a person, doesn't give you the right to use another person's bone marrow even if you need to use it.

And there's nothing particularly special about bone marrow. Suppose McFall had needed one of Shimp's kidneys or one of his lungs. If you agree it would have been wrong for the state to force Shimp to give McFall some of his bone marrow, I assume you'll also agree it would have been wrong for the state to force Shimp to give McFall one of his kidneys or one of his lungs. And if you agree the reason it would be wrong for the state to do this in the case of Shimp's bone marrow is that McFall had no right to use it, I assume you'll agree this is also why it would be wrong for the state to do this in the case of one of Shimp's kidneys or lungs. The crucial lesson we can draw from the case of *McFall v. Shimp*, then, isn't just a lesson about a person's right to control their bone marrow. It's a lesson about a person's right to control their body.

The lesson is this: the fact that someone is a person with a right to life doesn't mean they have the right to use another person's body even if they need to use that person's body in order to go on living. A person's right to life doesn't include the right to use another person's body, it doesn't entail the right to use another person's body, and it doesn't imply the right to use another person's body. From the fact that a person has a right to life, it doesn't follow that they have a right to use another person's body even if they need to use it. This fundamental proposition must be true if the case of *McFall v. Shimp* was decided correctly. So if you agree that it would have been wrong for the state to force Shimp to let McFall use his bone marrow in that case, you must agree that this fundamental proposition is true.

With this important lesson in mind, we can now see what the case of *McFall v. Shimp* has to do with the story of Alice. Alice was raped and now she's pregnant. We're assuming the fetus Alice is pregnant with is a person. So let's give the fetus a name. Let's call him Al. If people who defend the pro-life position are correct, Al has a right to life. For the purposes of this book, I'm simply assuming this is true. Defenders of the pro-life position then claim that because the fetus has a right to life, abortion is murder and should therefore be illegal. But the lesson we just learned from the case of *McFall v. Shimp* can now help us see that this is a mistake. As we saw in that case, the fact that Robert McFall had a right to life didn't mean he had a right to use another person's body to preserve his life. But if that's true in the case of McFall and Shimp, it must be true in the case of Al and Alice, too. Either having a right to life is enough to give you the right to use another person's body when you need to use it or it isn't.

Even if Al has a right to life, then, that doesn't give Al the right to use Alice's body even if he needs to use it. If having a right to life was enough to give Al the right to use Alice's body, after all, then having a right to life would have been enough to give McFall the right to use Shimp's body. And it wasn't enough to give McFall the right to use Shimp's body. So Al's right to life doesn't include the right to use Alice's body even if he needs to use it. The state had no right to force Shimp to let McFall use his body because McFall had no right to use Shimp's body. In the same way, and for the same reason, the fact that Al has a right to life—and I'm simply assuming for the sake of the argument that this is a fact—doesn't mean Al has the right to use Alice's body. And if Al has no right to use Alice's body, then the state has no right to force Alice to let Al use her body.

But if the state has no right to force Alice to let Al use her body, then the state has no right to force Alice to carry her pregnancy to term. And if the state has no right to force Alice to carry her pregnancy to term, then it has no right to prevent her from having an abortion. All this is true even if we assume Al is a person with a right to life. After all, the state had no right to force Shimp to let McFall use his body, and McFall was clearly a person with a right to life. So if you agree that it would be wrong for the state to force Shimp to let McFall use his bone marrow, you should also agree that abortion should be legal, at least in the case of rape, even if every fetus is a person with a right to life.

And it isn't just that you should think it should be legal for Alice to have an abortion in this case even if you think Al is a person. You should also think it should be legal for Alice to have an abortion in this case even if you think it would be immoral for Alice to have an abortion in this case. After all, you might think Shimp's refusal to let McFall have some of his bone marrow was immoral. Judge Flaherty certainly thought so. He called Shimp's behavior "morally indefensible." But the question before the judge wasn't "Would it be wrong for Shimp to refuse to let McFall use his body?" The question was "Would it be okay for the state to force Shimp to let McFall use his body if Shimp doesn't want to let McFall use it?" Judge Flaherty thought it was clear that Shimp was acting immorally, but he also thought it was clear the state had no business forcing Shimp not to act that way. So I'm not making any assumptions here about whether you think Shimp was acting immorally in refusing to let McFall use his body. Maybe you think he was and maybe you think he wasn't. The only assumption I'm making is that you think it would have been wrong for the state to force Shimp to let McFall use his body once Shimp decided he didn't want to let McFall use it.

This means when I try to argue from your belief about *McFall v. Shimp* to my claim about abortion, I'm not trying to draw any conclusions about whether it would be immoral for Alice to have an abortion, either. Maybe it would be immoral for Alice to have an abortion and maybe it wouldn't. My claim is simply that, regardless of whether it would be immoral for Alice to have an abortion, it would be wrong for the state to prevent her from having an abortion if that's what she decided she wanted to do. The goal of this book is to convince you that abortion should be legal, not to convince you that abortion isn't immoral.

Now, people who are pro-choice sometimes say things like this: "I'm personally opposed to abortion, but I think it should be the woman's choice." When people who are pro-choice say things like this, people who are pro-life sometimes complain that what they're saying is inconsistent or hypocritical. If you really think abortion is immoral, they respond, you should also think abortion should be illegal. But the case of *McFall v. Shimp* shows that this is a mistake, too. There's nothing inconsistent or hypocritical about saying it would be immoral for Shimp not to let McFall use his body while at the same time saying the state should let Shimp choose. In the same way, and for the same reason, there's nothing inconsistent or hypocritical about saying it would be immoral for Alice not to let Al use her body while at the same time saying the state should let Alice choose.

One important feature of this book is that it aims to convince you that abortion should be legal even if you think every fetus is a person with a right to life. This is what creates the possibility that we might resolve the debate over whether abortion should be legal without first having to get everyone to agree about whether the fetus is a person. But another important feature of this book is that it aims to convince you that abortion should be legal even if you think abortion is immoral. This creates the possibility that we might resolve the debate over whether abortion should be legal without first having to get everyone to agree about whether abortion is immoral, too. That's another reason to give the position I'm defending here a careful hearing even if you think the chances for success at the outset seem slim.

# 3

## Changing the Case

Have I already convinced you it should be legal for Alice to have an abortion after she was raped even if Al's a person? Probably not. I hope I've convinced you that the fact that Al has a right to life can't be enough by itself to give him the right to use Alice's body. After all, if having a right to life were enough to give Al the right to use Alice's body, then the fact that McFall had a right to life would have been enough to give McFall the right to use Shimp's body. And I'm assuming you agree it wasn't enough to give McFall that right.

But maybe Al still has the right to use Alice's body even though McFall didn't have the right to use Shimp's body because of some other fact about Alice's situation, some fact that makes Alice's situation different from Shimp's. If there turns out to be a difference between Alice and Shimp that makes a difference in this way, then thinking it would be wrong for the state to force Shimp to let McFall use his body won't commit you to thinking it would be wrong for the state to force Alice to let Al use her body. And if that turns out to be the case, the argument I'm trying to defend in this book will turn out to be unsuccessful.

Here's an example. McFall wasn't already using Shimp's body when the court was asked to intervene. But if the state prevents Alice from having an abortion, it does this after Al has already started using Alice's body. In *McFall v. Shimp*, that is, the court refused to force Shimp to let McFall start using his body to keep

McFall alive. But if the state forbids Alice from having an abortion, it wouldn't force Alice to let Al *start* using her body to keep Al alive. Instead, it would force Alice to let Al *continue* using her body to keep Al alive. That's a difference. If you think Judge Flaherty made the right call in *McFall v. Shimp* but you aren't yet convinced it should be legal for Alice to have an abortion even if Al's a person, you might be responding to this difference between the two cases.

Suppose this difference between the two cases is bothering you. You're wondering whether it poses a problem for my argument. Here's what you should do. You should make up your own story about McFall and Shimp. It should be just like the real story except in your version of the story, Shimp should discover that McFall is already using his body to go on living, just like Alice discovers that Al is already using her body to go on living. You should then ask whether you think this change in the story makes a difference. Would it be okay for the state to force Shimp to let McFall continue using his bone marrow in this version of the story?

If your answer to this question turns out to be yes, this will show you think the difference between the state's forcing someone to let another person start using their body and the state's forcing someone to let another person continue using their body really does make a difference. And if you think that, you should reject the argument I've offered here. But if your answer to this question turns out to be no, and you think it would still be wrong for the state to force Shimp to let McFall use his body even if McFall had already started using Shimp's body, this will show you think the difference between the state's forcing someone to let another person start using their body and the state's forcing someone to let another person continue using their body doesn't really make a difference. And if you think this difference between the case of McFall and Shimp and the case of Al and Alice doesn't make a difference, then you should reject this first objection to the argument I've offered here. If the difference between the cases doesn't make a difference, then as long as you agree it would be wrong for the state to force Shimp to let McFall use his bone marrow, you'll still have to agree it would be wrong for the state to force Alice to let Al use her uterus.

Since this approach to evaluating the merits of my argument may be unfamiliar to you, I'll go ahead and give you an example you can use here. If you don't like the example, feel free to come up with one of your own; any good example should produce the same results. In any event, here's one way you can change the story of McFall and Shimp to test this first objection to my argument. Suppose on the day after the judge ruled in Shimp's favor a distraught friend of McFall's slipped a drug into Shimp's coffee that rendered Shimp unconscious. Suppose while Shimp was unconscious this friend of McFall's then connected Shimp to a device that started slowly extracting bone marrow from Shimp and transferring it to McFall. I'll call this device a bone marrow transferring machine. Suppose when Shimp woke up, he discovered that due to no fault of his own, his bone marrow was already being used to keep McFall alive. And suppose Shimp decided he didn't want to let McFall continue to use his bone marrow.

This change to the story makes the case of McFall and Shimp more like the case of Al and Alice. It certainly doesn't make the case of McFall and Shimp exactly like the case of Al and Alice. There are plenty of other differences between the two cases, and I'll get to them later. But this change to the story does make the case of McFall and Shimp just like the case of Al and Alice in terms of the one specific difference I want to focus on right now: the difference between the state's forcing someone to let another person start using their body and the state's forcing someone to let another person continue using their body. Someone slips a drug into Alice's coffee, and when she wakes up Al is already using her body to go on living. Someone slips a drug into Shimp's coffee, and when he wakes up McFall is already using his body to go on living. It's not Al's fault that he's now using Alice's body to go on living. But it's not McFall's fault that he's now using Shimp's body to go on living, either. In fact, if it helps, let's assume from here on out that McFall has lapsed into a temporary coma because of his condition and that he is just as innocent and helpless as Al is. So at least in terms of this particular difference, this revised version of the story of McFall and Shimp is just like the case of Al and Alice.

Now, suppose that after Shimp wakes up and says he's not willing to allow McFall to continue using his body, McFall's lawyer rushes back to the courthouse and asks Judge Flaherty to intervene. And suppose McFall's lawyer says something like this: "Look, your Honor, I admit it really would have been wrong for you to force Mr. Shimp to let my client start using his bone marrow yesterday. But things have changed. Today, my client is already using Mr. Shimp's bone marrow. All I'm asking this time is that you force Mr. Shimp to let my client *continue* to use it. Surely there'd be nothing wrong with your doing that."

I doubt you'll find this position plausible. If you agreed with Judge Flaherty's position in the real case of *McFall v. Shimp*, I bet you'll think the judge should say the same thing in this fictional version of the case. It's hard to see why anyone would think it would be wrong for the state to force Shimp to start helping McFall but okay for the state to force Shimp to continue helping McFall if Shimp woke up and found out his body was already being used to keep McFall alive in this way. If McFall had no right to use Shimp's bone marrow to begin with, why would McFall suddenly have this right simply because someone slipped a drug into Shimp's coffee and hooked him up to the bone marrow transferring machine? And if you agree that it would be wrong for the state to force Shimp to keep McFall alive in this fictional version of the story, you should reject this first objection to my argument. If the fact that someone forced Shimp to let McFall start using his body isn't enough to give McFall the right to continue using Shimp's body, then the fact that someone forced Alice to start letting Al use her body can't be enough to give Al the right to continue using Alice's body, either. The fact that Shimp's body wasn't yet keeping McFall alive in the real-life version of the story while Alice's body is already keeping Al alive in the case of Alice's unwanted pregnancy therefore turns out to be irrelevant. So this first difference between the two cases provides no reason for you to reject the claim I've made so far: if you agree that it would be wrong for the state to force Shimp to let McFall use his bone marrow, you should agree that it would be wrong for the state to force Alice to let Al use her uterus. Even if Al is a person with a right to life, it should be legal for Alice to have an abortion.

# 4

## Hypothetical Cases

I began this book by describing something that actually happened. Robert McFall really did need some of David Shimp's bone marrow and David Shimp really did refuse to give it to him. McFall really did ask the court to force Shimp to give him the bone marrow he needed and the court really did say no. I then said I was going to try to convince you that if you think it would be wrong for the state to force Shimp to let McFall use his bone marrow in this case, you should also think abortion should be legal even if every fetus is a person with a right to life. And I turned to the case of Alice to try to convince you this is true at least in the case of pregnancies arising from rape.

But here we are just a few pages later, and I've already changed the story of McFall and Shimp from something that actually happened to something bizarrely different. As far as I know, there's no such thing as a bone marrow transferring machine; I just made it up. For all I know, there will never be such a machine. Maybe there's even something about bone marrow that makes it impossible for a machine like that to exist. I don't know. In responding to the first objection to the argument I've offered here, then, it seems I've moved quite suddenly from historical fact to science fiction. And you might think this is a problem. That's because you might think it's reasonable for me to appeal to what you believe about something that actually happened but not reasonable for me to appeal to what you would believe about something that never happened and that, for all I know, will never happen and maybe even couldn't ever happen. I began by saying I'd try to convince you that if you agree with what Judge Flaherty actually said, you should agree that abortion should be legal. But now I seem to be saying something quite different: that if you agree with something Judge Flaherty said in a strange make-believe story, then you should agree that abortion should be legal. And that seems to be another matter entirely.

Here's what's going on: I'm making an assumption. I'm assuming it's okay for me to appeal to your beliefs about cases that are purely hypothetical, even if the cases are somewhat strange or bizarre, and not just to your beliefs about actual, real-life cases. This is a pretty common practice among philosophers, though not so much among other people. Some people don't think this is a reasonable assumption. I think it is. Here's why I think you should, too. Suppose you reject my assumption. You agree it's okay for me to appeal to your beliefs about actual cases but you say it's not okay for me to appeal to your beliefs about strange, imaginary cases. So you agree that if your belief about the actual case of *McFall v. Shimp* turns out to commit you to saying abortion should be legal, then you really have to agree that abortion should be legal. But you claim that if it's merely your belief about my strange, imaginary version of the case that turns out to commit you to saying abortion should be legal, then this doesn't really mean you have to agree that abortion should be legal.

If that's your view, you should consider that your view has a very strange implication. It implies that whether abortion should be legal depends on whether the original case of *McFall v. Shimp* that I described is something that actually happened or just a strange story I made up. Now I've told you, of course, that the case of *McFall v. Shimp* is something that actually happened. But you don't really know that for a fact. Chances are pretty good you never heard of the case before you opened this book. So for all you know, maybe I really did just make it up. Now suppose someone asks if you think abortion should be legal. If you start out thinking abortion should be illegal, and if you find no fault with anything else I say in this book but you insist it's only fair for me to appeal to your beliefs about actual cases and not to your beliefs about strange hypothetical cases, then you'll have to answer this question by saying something like this: "I don't know if abortion should be legal because I don't know if the case of *McFall v. Shimp* really happened. If it really happened, then abortion should be legal, but if it's just a strange, made-up story, then abortion should be illegal." I hope you'll agree this would be an unsatisfactory answer. How could the state's right to force a woman to carry her pregnancy to term depend on whether Robert McFall really tried to get the state to force his cousin to let him have some of his bone marrow? If you agree this implication is unacceptable, then you have to reject the claim that has this implication. If you reject the claim that has this implication, you'll have to agree that it's okay for me to appeal to your beliefs about strange, imaginary cases, and not just to your beliefs about actual, real-life cases, as I try to convince you that abortion should be legal. And that's what I'm going to do in much of what follows.

# 5

## Contraceptive Failure

Barbara is a 19-year-old college student in Boston. A few weeks ago, she had sex with a guy she met at a party. She didn't want to get pregnant, so she insisted that he use a condom. Unfortunately for Barbara, the condom broke that night, and she's just discovered she's pregnant. To help us keep track of which fetus is Alice's and which fetus is Barbara's, let's call Barbara's fetus Bob. Although Barbara really hoped she wouldn't get pregnant, she knew she might because she knew that condoms sometimes break. And she went ahead and had sex with the guy she met at the party despite knowing this because she thought having sex with the guy would be fun. It was fun, but now she's pregnant with Bob and she wants an abortion. Should the state let her have one?

Barbara's relationship to Bob seems importantly different from Alice's relationship to Al. Alice didn't do anything to cause herself to get pregnant with Al. She was raped. But Barbara did do something to cause herself to get pregnant with Bob. She chose to have sex with the guy she met at the party. And even though Barbara tried to prevent this choice from causing her to get pregnant, she knew it might cause her to get pregnant all the same. And she chose to have sex with the guy anyway. This seems like a big difference.

Barbara's situation also seems importantly different from Shimp's situation. In the somewhat strange version of Shimp's story that I used to try to convince you it should be legal for Alice to have an abortion, Shimp was like Alice and unlike Barbara in this respect. Shimp didn't do anything to cause himself to end up in the predicament he found himself in, either. He simply woke up one day and discovered that his body was being used to keep someone else alive. That's what happened to Alice. But it's not what happened to Barbara. Barbara did something that caused her to end up in the predicament she finds herself in and she did what she did knowing full well that doing it might cause her to end up in just such a predicament. Again, this seems like a big difference.

These differences between Barbara's situation and the situations of Alice and Shimp seem to show that the argument I've defended here, if it works at all, can only work in cases involving rape. I'm counting on you to think it would be wrong for the state to force Shimp to remain connected to the bone marrow transferring machine in the version of the story where Shimp is drugged and connected to the machine against his will, that is, and I've suggested that the case of Alice is relevantly similar to this version of the story. If I'm right about that, then your belief about Shimp in this version of the story commits you to believing the state should let Alice have an abortion even if Al is a person with a right to life.

But even if I turn out to be right about that, what I've said so far clearly doesn't apply to the case of Barbara. I can't say that if you think it would be wrong for the state to force Shimp to let McFall continue using his bone marrow in this case then you have to think it would be wrong for the state to force Barbara to let Bob continue using her uterus because there's a big difference between Shimp's situation and Barbara's situation. It's not Shimp's fault he finds himself keeping McFall alive, just as it's not Alice's fault she finds herself keeping Al alive, but it seems plausible to say that it's Barbara's fault that she finds herself keeping Bob alive. And that may be enough to show that Barbara shouldn't be allowed to have an abortion even if Alice should be allowed to have one.

Now the fact that Bob has a right to life can't be enough to show he has a right to use Barbara's body. If Bob's right to life were enough to give him the right to use Barbara's body, after all, then McFall's right to life would have been enough to give him the right to use Shimp's body. And McFall's right to life wasn't enough to give him the right to use Shimp's body. But even though Bob's right to life can't be enough to give Bob the right to use Barbara's body, the fact that Bob has a right to life plus the fact that it's Barbara's fault that he started using her body might be enough to give him that right. And since it wasn't Shimp's fault that McFall started using his bone marrow and it isn't Alice's fault that Al started using her uterus, this would mean you could say Bob has the right to use Barbara's body without having to say McFall had the right to use Shimp's body or that Al has the right to use Alice's body. And this, in turn, would mean that even if I can use the case of McFall and Shimp to show it should be legal for Alice to have an abortion after she was raped, I can't use it to show it should be legal for Barbara to have an abortion after she freely chose to have sex with the guy she met at a party.

This looks like a problem for my argument. But I think it can be overcome. The way to do that is to change the story of McFall and Shimp again. What we need this time is an imaginary version of the story that's like the real case of McFall and Shimp, except this time Shimp's situation will have to be like Barbara's situation instead of like Alice's situation in this respect. We need a version of the story, that is, where Shimp doesn't simply wake up and discover that his body is being used to keep McFall alive. We need a version of the story where Shimp freely chooses to do something knowing full well that if he does it, it might cause him to end up in a situation where his body is being used to keep

McFall alive. In short, we need a version of the story where, just as it's Barbara's fault that Bob started using her body, it's Shimp's fault that McFall started using his body. This will undoubtedly make for an even stranger story. But as I already said, I'm assuming at this point you're okay with my appealing to your beliefs about such stories.

If we can come up with a suitable test case, one that's like the case of Barbara rather than like the case of Alice in this respect, we can ask whether we think it would be okay for the state to force Shimp to continue to keep McFall alive in this new version of the story. If you think the answer to this question is yes, then the problem with my argument will remain. If it would be okay for the state to force Shimp to keep McFall alive in a situation that really is like Barbara's situation, then it would be okay for the state to force Barbara to keep Bob alive and so okay for the state to prevent her from having an abortion. But if you think the answer to this question is no, then what at first seemed like a problem with my argument will turn out not to be a problem after all. If it would still be wrong for the state to force Shimp to continue to keep McFall alive even if Shimp's situation really were like Barbara's situation rather than like Alice's, then it would be wrong for the state to prevent Barbara from having an abortion, too, and not just wrong for the state to prevent Alice from having one. And it would be wrong for the state to do this to Barbara even if Bob is a person, since it would be wrong for the state to do this to Shimp even though McFall was a person. What we need, then, is a better version of the story of McFall and Shimp to apply to the case of Bob and Barbara—one where it's Shimp's fault that McFall is already using his bone marrow.

Here's one way to make the story of McFall and Shimp like the case of Barbara and unlike the case of Alice in this respect. Feel free again to supply your own example if you don't like this one. Suppose a few days after telling McFall he was unwilling to let him use some of his bone marrow, Shimp went down to the hospital to visit him. Suppose when Shimp got there, McFall had already been hooked up to a bone marrow transferring machine in the hope that Shimp might change his mind. Suppose, in addition, the floor in McFall's room had recently been cleaned, washed, and polished and was extremely slippery as a result. Before Shimp entered the room, in fact, he was warned: "The floor in there is extremely slippery. If you walk in there, you might slip and fall and get stuck to the bone marrow transferring machine. And if that happens, it will start removing some of your bone marrow and transferring it to McFall." Suppose Shimp decided to take his chances despite this warning just because he thought it would be fun to visit his cousin. He put on special non-slip shoes and tried to walk very slowly, but he still ended up slipping and falling and getting stuck to the machine. As a result, Shimp is now lying on the floor next to McFall and the machine is removing some of his bone marrow and giving it to McFall.

I admit this is an extremely peculiar story, perhaps one only a philosopher would dream up. But I'm going to ask you to think about it anyway. The reason I'm going to ask you to think about it is that this version of the story of McFall and Shimp, strange as it certainly is, manages to make Shimp's situation just like Barbara's situation, and unlike Alice's situation, in this one very particular respect: it makes Shimp's situation like Barbara's situation in terms of whether or not the person whose body is currently being used to keep someone else alive freely chose to do something that foreseeably caused them to end up in such a predicament. Alice was raped while she was unconscious. She did nothing to cause her predicament. And Shimp did nothing to cause his predicament in the fictional version of the case that I compared to Alice. But Barbara did do something that caused her predicament: she freely chose to have sex with the guy she met at a party, knowing that doing so might cause her to end up in a situation where someone else was now making use of her body to go on living. And in this newest version of Shimp's story, Shimp did something that caused his predicament, too: he freely chose to walk across the slippery floor knowing it might cause him to be in a situation where someone else was now making use of his body to go on living. Barbara took precautions to prevent her from ending up in such a situation. But so did Shimp.

Now suppose you agree that the fact that Bob is a person who needs to use Barbara's body isn't enough to give Bob the right to use Barbara's body. Remember, you have to agree that this fact isn't enough to give Bob the right to use Barbara's body if you agree that the fact that McFall was a person who needed to use Shimp's body wasn't enough to give McFall the right to use Shimp's body in the real-life version of that case. But suppose you also think this fact plus the fact that it's Barbara's fault that Bob's now using her body really is enough to give Bob the right to continue using her body. If that turns out to be the case, then Bob will have the right to use Barbara's body even if Al doesn't have the right to use Alice's body. And that would mean it should be illegal for Barbara to have an abortion after she freely chose to have sex with that guy even if it shouldn't be illegal for Alice to have an abortion after she was raped.

But if this is what you're thinking about Bob and Barbara, you'll have to say that McFall has the right to continue using Shimp's body in this new version of the story. After all, McFall is a person and McFall needs to use Shimp's body to go on living, and in this new version of the story it's Shimp's fault that McFall is now using his body. If you think it would be okay for the state to prevent Barbara from having an abortion because it's Barbara's fault her body is now being used to keep someone else alive, then you'll have to agree that it would also be okay for the state to force Shimp to let McFall continue using his body in this new version of the story because it's Shimp's fault his body is now being used to keep someone else alive. Either the fact that it's your fault someone else is using your body to stay alive is enough to give them the right to continue using it or it isn't. That's why, as strange as this new version of the story surely is, you really do have to think about it if you want to figure out whether the fact that it's Barbara's fault that Bob is now using her body is enough to make it okay for the state to prevent Barbara from having an abortion.

So go ahead and think about it. Would it be okay for the state to force Shimp to let McFall continue using his bone marrow in this version of the story? If you think it would be okay for the state to force Shimp to let McFall continue using his bone marrow in this version of the story, then I'll have to admit my strategy here has failed. But my guess is very few people will think this. If you agree with Judge Flaherty's decision in the real case of *McFall v. Shimp*, as I'm assuming you do, then you agree it would be wrong for the state to force Shimp to let McFall start using some of his bone marrow. And if you agree it would be wrong for the state to force Shimp to let McFall start using some of his bone marrow, it's hard to see how you could think it would be okay for the state to force Shimp to let McFall continue using some of his bone marrow just because Shimp accidentally ended up starting to let McFall use some of it. If McFall had no right to use Shimp's bone marrow to begin with, why would McFall suddenly have this right simply because Shimp slipped on the floor and got stuck to the bone marrow transferring machine? If you were the one who slipped on the floor and accidentally got stuck to the machine, I doubt you'd think this gave the state the right to force you to remain attached to it.

So I suspect that upon reflection you'll agree the state wouldn't have the right to force Shimp to let McFall continue to use his bone marrow in the admittedly peculiar version of the story I've described here. You'll agree it would be wrong for the state to do this even though McFall is a person, McFall needs Shimp's bone marrow, and Shimp could have avoided letting McFall start to use his bone marrow by not walking into the room in the first place. And if that's right, then you can't say Bob has the right to use Barbara's body just because Bob's a person, Bob needs to use Barbara's body, and Barbara could have avoided letting Bob start to use her body by not having sex with the guy she met at the party in the first place. Either the fact that it's your fault someone has started to use your body is enough to give them the right to keep using it if they need to keep using it or it isn't. If it's not enough to give them this right in this version of the case of McFall and Shimp, then it's not enough to give them this right in the case of Bob and Barbara. If it would be wrong for the state to prevent Alice from having an abortion after she was raped, then it would also be wrong for the state to prevent Barbara from having an abortion after she freely chose to have sex with that guy. It's Barbara's fault that Bob started using her body while it isn't Alice's fault that Al started using her body, but the modified version of the story of McFall and Shimp shows that this difference doesn't make a difference in terms of whether the state should allow them to have abortions.

I've covered a lot of ground already. It may help to briefly review what I've tried to do so far. I started by assuming you agree with Judge Flaherty's decision in the real-life case of *McFall v. Shimp*. It would be wrong for the state to force Shimp to let McFall use his bone marrow in that case, even though McFall was a person and McFall needed the bone marrow. I then tried to convince you of a few things based on this assumption. First, that if it would be wrong for the state to do this to Shimp in the real case of McFall and Shimp, then it would also be wrong for the state to do this to Shimp in a fictional version of the case where someone rendered Shimp unconscious and started using his bone marrow to keep McFall alive against his will. Second, if it would be wrong for the state to do this to Shimp in this fictional version of the story, then it would also be wrong for the state to prevent Alice from having an abortion when she becomes pregnant as the result of rape. Third, if it would be wrong for the state to do this to Shimp in the real case of McFall and Shimp, then it would also be wrong for the state to do this to Shimp in a second fictional version of the story where Shimp slips on the floor and accidentally starts supplying McFall with some of his bone marrow. Fourth, if it would be wrong for the state to do this to Shimp in this second fictional version of the story, then it would also be wrong for the state to prevent Barbara from having an abortion when she accidentally becomes pregnant because the condom broke.

If I've been right about all this, then if you agree with Judge Flaherty's decision in the real-life case of *McFall v. Shimp*, you should also agree that it would be wrong for the state to ban abortion at least in cases where the pregnant woman was raped and in cases where the pregnant woman had sex voluntarily while unsuccessfully using birth control. Since you agree it would be wrong for the state to force Shimp to keep McFall alive even though McFall was a person with a right to life, you should agree it would be wrong for the state to force a pregnant woman to carry her pregnancy to term in these cases even if you think the fetus is also a person with a right to life. And since you might think Shimp's refusal to keep McFall alive is immoral in these cases even though it would be wrong for the state to force Shimp to keep McFall alive, you should agree it would be wrong for the state to prevent Alice and Barbara from having abortions in these cases even if you think it would be immoral for them to have abortions in these cases.

Some defenses of the claim that abortion should be legal depend on the claim that the fetus isn't really a person or on the claim that abortion isn't immoral. But the defense of abortion rights I've offered here doesn't depend on either of these claims.

Even if you think Al and Bob have a right to life, and even if you think it would be immoral for Alice and Barbara to refuse to let them use their bodies to go on living, you should still agree that it would be wrong for the state to prevent them from making that choice if that's the choice they decide to make. Or, at least, that's what you should think if you agree it would be wrong for the state to prevent Shimp from making the choice not to let McFall use some of his bone marrow.

# 6

## Failure to Use Contraception

Carol is a 37-year-old cocktail waitress in Reno. She had sex with her ex-boyfriend a couple months ago. She didn't want to get pregnant, and she didn't have any birth control with her at the time, but she wanted to be spontaneous. So she decided to take her chances. She figured if she got pregnant, she could always have an abortion. Why worry about finding a condom, she said, when you can always use abortion as your form of birth control. Unfortunately for Carol, she got pregnant that night, and a second test has just confirmed this. She has no interest in keeping the child, let alone giving him a name, but to help us keep track of the different cases, let's call him Carl. Should the state let Carol have an abortion? Or does Carl have the right to use Carol's uterus?

In many respects, Carol's situation is like Barbara's. Unlike Alice, who was raped, Barbara and Carol each freely chose to have sex with someone knowing full well that doing so could get them pregnant. I've already tried to convince you it would be wrong for the state to prevent Barbara from having an abortion. If that's right, and if Carol's situation is basically the same as Barbara's, then it would be wrong for the state to prevent Carol from having an abortion, too. But there's also a difference between Barbara and Carol. While both of them knew they were running the risk of getting pregnant, Barbara tried to do something to minimize that risk while Carol didn't. Barbara insisted on using birth control. She just got unlucky. Carol, on the other hand, did nothing to reduce her chances of getting pregnant even though she knew she could have done something. In this respect, Carol seems more responsible for her predicament than Barbara is for hers. And you might think this should make a difference. Even if you agree that Alice and Barbara should be allowed to have an abortion, you might be tempted to draw the line at Carol. That's because you might think, as many people put it, that abortion shouldn't be used as a form of birth control.

How can we figure out if this is a reasonable thing to say? By now, you can probably guess how I'm going to answer that question. We can figure out whether this is a reasonable thing to say by changing the story about McFall and Shimp yet again. This time, we need to make Shimp's situation less like Barbara's and more like Carol's. In the imaginary version of Shimp's story I compared to Barbara's situation, Shimp walked into McFall's slippery hospital room knowing that doing so might cause him to end up getting stuck to McFall's bone marrow transferring machine. Even though he put on special nonslip shoes and tried to walk very slowly, Shimp still ended up slipping and falling and getting stuck to the machine. I'm assuming at this point you agree it would be wrong for the state to force Shimp to let McFall continue using his bone marrow in this version of the story even though he knew the precautions he was taking might turn out to fail. And I've tried to convince you that if that's so, then you should also agree it would be wrong for the state to force Barbara to let Bob continue using her body even though she knew the precautions she was taking might turn out to fail, too. If the fact that it's Shimp's fault that McFall started using his bone marrow doesn't give McFall the right to continue using it, then the fact that it's Barbara's fault that Bob started using her uterus doesn't give Bob the right to continue using it.

But what about Carol? Carol's situation is like Barbara's, except Carol didn't take any precautions to avoid getting pregnant while Barbara did. So the way to change the imaginary story about Shimp that I compared to Barbara's situation is to have Shimp fail to take precautions to avoid letting McFall start using his bone marrow. After he's warned about the slippery floor in McFall's room, for example, suppose instead of putting on special nonslip shoes and walking very slowly, Shimp decided it would be more fun to spontaneously race across the room in his socks, and that's why he slipped and fell and ended up getting stuck to the bone marrow transferring machine. In this version of the story, Shimp seems more responsible for the fact that McFall has started using his bone marrow than he was in the version where he wore special nonslip shoes and walked very slowly. This seems true in the same way that Carol seems more responsible for the fact that Carl has started using her uterus than Barbara was for the fact that Bob had started using her uterus because Barbara, unlike Carol, was careful to use birth control. So the version of the story where Shimp races across the slippery floor in his socks seems to be the right one to compare to Carol's situation.

Let's suppose that's right. What do you think about this version of the story? Should the state have the right to force Shimp to let McFall continue using his bone marrow in this case? Should the fact that Shimp could have reduced his chances of slipping and falling by wearing the special nonslip shoes and walking very slowly make a difference? If you think it would be okay for the state to force Shimp to let McFall continue using his bone marrow in this case, then you really should draw the line at Carol. You should agree it would be wrong for the state to prevent Alice and Barbara from having an abortion. But you should conclude that it would be okay for the state to prevent Carol from having an abortion since Carol could have reduced her chances of having

Carl start using her uterus by using birth control. Or, at least, you should think this if you think Carl is a person.

But my guess is very few people will think it would be okay for the state to do this to Shimp even in this version of the story. If you agree with Judge Flaherty's decision in the real case of *McFall v. Shimp*, as I'm assuming you do, then you agree it would be wrong for the state to force Shimp to let McFall start using some of his bone marrow. And if you agree it would be wrong for the state to force Shimp to let McFall start using some of his bone marrow, it's hard to see how you could think it would be okay for the state to force Shimp to let McFall continue using some of his bone marrow just because he accidentally ended up letting McFall start to use some of it when he could have reduced the chances of this accidentally happening by wearing special nonslip shoes and walking more slowly. If McFall had no right to use Shimp's bone marrow to begin with, why would McFall suddenly have this right simply because Shimp's slipping on the floor was due to his own reckless behavior? If you were the one who slipped on the floor because you decided to run across it in your socks, I doubt you'd think that the fact that you could have been more careful would give the state the right to force you to remain attached to the bone marrow transferring machine you now found yourself stuck to. And so I suspect that, at least upon reflection, you'll agree the state wouldn't have the right to force Shimp to let McFall continue using his bone marrow in the version of the story I've described here, even though Shimp could have reduced his chances of winding up in a situation where someone else was using his body to go on living by wearing the special nonslip shoes and walking more slowly.

If I'm right about this and you agree that the fact that Shimp could have done more to prevent McFall from starting to use his bone marrow doesn't mean McFall now has the right to continue using it, you'll have to agree that the fact that Carol could have done more to prevent Carl from starting to use her uterus doesn't mean Carl now has the right to continue using it. Either the fact that someone could have done more to prevent another person from starting to use their body to go on living is enough to give that other person the right to continue using their body or it isn't. And the fact that Carl has a right to life doesn't give him the right to use Carol's body either because if it did, then the fact that McFall had a right to life would have given McFall the right to use Shimp's body in the real-life version of the case. So the fact that Carl has a right to life doesn't give him the right to use Carol's body, the fact that it's Carol's fault that she accidentally let Carl start using her body doesn't give him the right to continue using her body, and the fact that she failed to take precautions to reduce the chances of that accidentally happening doesn't give him the right to use her body, either. There's a difference between the case of Carol and the case of Barbara, then, but this further modified version of the story of McFall and Shimp shows that the difference doesn't matter in terms of whether it would be okay for the state to prevent them from having an abortion. And if that's right, then you should agree that it would be wrong for the state to prevent Carol from having an abortion even though she could have reduced the chances of winding up in her predicament by finding some birth control before she had sex with her ex-boyfriend.

So, it should be legal for a woman to have an abortion if her pregnancy is the result of rape, it should be legal for a woman to have an abortion if her pregnancy is the result of contraceptive failure, and it should be legal for a woman to have an abortion if her pregnancy is the result of freely choosing to engage in unprotected sex. This is what you should think if you agree with Judge Flaherty's decision in the versions of the story of *McFall v. Shimp* I've appealed to here. Since you agree it would be wrong for the state to force Shimp to keep McFall alive in these cases even though McFall was a person with a right to life, you should agree it would be wrong for the state to force a woman to carry her pregnancy to term in these cases even if you think every fetus is a person with a right to life. And since you agree it would be wrong for the state to force Shimp to keep McFall alive in these cases even if you think Shimp's refusal to keep McFall alive in these cases would be immoral, you should agree it would be wrong for the state to prevent Alice, Barbara, and Carol from having abortions in the cases I've described even if you think it would be immoral for them to have abortions in these cases.

# 7

## Sex Selection

Dorothy and her husband live in Cleveland. They've been happily married for five years now and have an adorable 2-year-old son. They'd like to have one more child before Dorothy goes back to work full time and they'd like it to be a girl. Nothing against boys, mind you. They'd just like to have one of each. Dorothy was recently excited to learn she's pregnant again, but testing has since confirmed it's a boy. She was hoping to have Danielle, but instead she's pregnant with Daniel. She and her husband only want to have one more child and they really want it to be a girl this time. So Dorothy is planning to have an abortion. Should the state let her have one?

Even people who are strongly pro-choice as a general matter are often made uncomfortable by the subject of sex-selection abortion. There's no reason to think large numbers of women are having abortions based on the sex of their fetus in this country so it can be tempting simply not to talk about it. But that would be a mistake for two reasons. First, unlike abortion in more typical cases, sex-selection abortion is illegal in parts of the United States right now. If Dorothy and her husband lived in Arizona, Kansas, North Dakota, South Dakota, Oklahoma, Pennsylvania, or North Carolina, she'd be out of luck. It would be illegal for her to get an abortion there. Second, even if relatively few women in this country want to get an abortion because of the sex of their fetus, a law that prevents them from doing so has an impact on all women who want to get an abortion. It means they all have to justify their decision to the government in a way they wouldn't otherwise have to.

Of course, if there's a good enough reason to ban abortion in these cases, the women who want them may just have to accept the consequences. But the reason I've given for thinking abortion should be legal in more typical cases applies just as plainly and forcefully here: the fact that a fetus is a person, assuming it is a fact, doesn't give it the right to use another person's body even if it needs to use it. This is true even if the person whose body the fetus needs to use refuses to let the fetus use it only because of the fetus's sex. After all, consider what happens if we tinker with the story of McFall and Shimp yet again and make it a sex-selection case, too.

Suppose Shimp would have been willing to let his cousin have some of his bone marrow if his cousin had been female. He finds himself connected to the bone marrow transferring machine because he slipped and fell onto it, but at first he doesn't complain. In fact, he says, he's happy to help out. But after he's been connected to the machine for a while, he takes a closer look at McFall and, with note of incredulity in his voice, utters the following words: "Wait a minute! *Robert* McFall? I thought you said it was *Roberta* McFall, his sister, who needed my bone marrow. I'd be willing to help Roberta out. She's a chick, and I'm a chivalrous kind of guy. Ladies first and all that. But *Robert* McFall? No way. He's a dude. Guys have to fend for themselves. So let me outta here." Suppose McFall's lawyer then asked the court to order Shimp to remain connected to the machine until McFall had received enough bone marrow from him and that the court refused to do so.

You might think it would be immoral for Shimp to refuse to let McFall have the bone marrow he needs in this case, given that

Shimp would have been willing to let McFall have it if McFall had been a woman instead of a man. And if you're like many people, you'll think that if Shimp were engaging in a commercial transaction of some sort it would be appropriate for the state to force him to treat his male and female employees or customers equally in a variety of ways. But if you agreed with Judge Flaherty in the actual case of *McFall v. Shimp*, I think you'll agree that if Shimp decides to let McFall have some of his bone marrow, he's doing something importantly different from what people do when they enter the public marketplace. He's simply giving McFall a gift. And in the case of giving people gifts, it's hard to believe you'll think it would be okay for the state to force people to treat men and women equally. If Shimp wants to give gifts to all his female friends and relatives and to none of his male friends or relatives, you might think that's morally objectionable, but I bet you'll think the law should let him do it. So even if you think Shimp's behavior is immoral in this version of the story, it's hard to believe you'll think the state should force Shimp to give McFall the bone marrow. If McFall didn't have the right to use Shimp's bone marrow in the real version of the case, why would McFall suddenly have this right just because Shimp would have been willing to donate the bone marrow to McFall if McFall had been a woman?

If you agree it would be wrong for the state to force Shimp to keep McFall alive even if the only reason Shimp refused to keep him alive was that McFall was male rather than female, then you should agree it would be wrong for the state to force Dorothy to keep Daniel alive even if the only reason she refuses to carry her pregnancy to term is that Daniel is male rather than female. I've already tried to convince you it should be legal for Alice, Barbara and Carol to have abortions. If you agreed with me about those cases, you should agree about the case of Dorothy, too. It should be legal for a woman to have an abortion regardless of how she got pregnant and regardless of whether sex selection plays a role in her decision. And you should agree that it should be legal for a woman to have an abortion because of the fetus's sex even if you think every fetus is a person with a right to life, and even if you think having an abortion because of the fetus's sex would be immoral.

# 8

## Genetic Screening

Elaine is a 43-year-old homemaker and mother of four who lives just outside Houston. When she and her husband found out she was pregnant again, they were surprised. Their youngest child is already 12 and they'd assumed Elaine was no longer fertile. Still, once they got over the initial shock and had some time to think about the implications for their family, they decided the news was an unexpected blessing and they began to prepare their home to welcome a fifth child, Evan. Then they found out Evan would have Down syndrome. After several long and anguished conversations, they agreed that it would be better if Elaine had an abortion. Should the state let her have one?

Abortions because of fetal abnormalities, like sex-selection abortions, make many defenders of abortion rights uncomfortable. Bans on such abortions are less common in the United States than bans on sex-selection abortions, but they do exist. It would be illegal for Elaine to have an abortion in North Dakota right now, for example, and Indiana and Louisiana have passed similar laws, though courts there have temporarily blocked them from going into effect. So this kind of case shouldn't be ignored, either. As was also the case with sex-selection abortions, the reason I've given here for thinking abortion should be legal in more typical cases applies just as clearly and forcefully to abortions based on fetal abnormality. And, again as was true in the case of sex-selection abortions, we can see this by once more reworking the story of McFall and Shimp.

So suppose again that Shimp finds himself connected to the bone marrow transferring machine after he slipped and fell onto it, and that he doesn't complain about this at first. But suppose this time when Shimp takes a closer look at his cousin, he discovers not that McFall is male rather than female but, instead, that McFall has Down syndrome. And suppose when he finds out, he says something like this: "You're telling me *that's* my cousin? The funny-looking guy? Why didn't anybody warn me? I never met my cousin before, but I thought he was normal. No way I'm letting this guy have any of my bone marrow. I can't even stand to look at him."

As objectionable as Shimp's attitude clearly is in this version of the story, it's hard to believe you'll think this would make it okay for the state to force him to stay hooked up to the bone marrow transferring machine. As in the case of sex-selection abortion, you may well agree that if Shimp were engaging in a commercial transaction of some sort it would be appropriate for the state to force him to treat all his employees or customers equally in a variety of ways, regardless of any disabilities they might have. But, again as in that case, it's hard to believe you'll think it would be okay for the state to force people to treat others equally in terms of disabilities when it comes to giving gifts. And if you agree with Judge Flaherty's decision in the real case of *McFall v. Shimp*, you'll agree that if Shimp decides to let McFall have some of his bone marrow, he's simply agreeing to offer him a gift. So if McFall didn't have the right to use Shimp's bone marrow in the real-life version of the story, why would McFall suddenly have this right simply because he had Down syndrome and because Shimp would have let him have the bone marrow if he hadn't had Down syndrome? If you agree that it would still be wrong for the state to force Shimp to keep McFall alive even if the only reason Shimp refused to keep him alive was that McFall had Down syndrome, then you should agree that it would be wrong for the state to force Elaine to keep Evan alive even if the only reason she refused to carry her pregnancy to term was that Evan had Down syndrome. As in the case of Dorothy's sex-selection abortion, you might think it would be immoral for Elaine to have an abortion for this reason. But, again as in the case of Dorothy's sex-selection abortion, if you agree it would be wrong for the state to force Shimp to let McFall use his bone marrow even though you object to Shimp's reason for not wanting to let McFall use it, you should agree it would be wrong for the state to force Elaine to let Evan use her uterus even though you object to Elaine's reason for not wanting to let Evan use it.

I've tried to convince you it should be legal for Alice, Barbara, Carol, and Dorothy to have abortions. If you agreed with me about those cases, you should agree about the case of Elaine, too. For that matter, you should agree it should be legal for Dorothy and Elaine to have abortions no matter how trivial their reason for wanting one is. Suppose the only reason Shimp was unwilling to donate bone marrow to McFall was that he had tickets to a Pirates game that he didn't want to miss. Even if you don't think Shimp's behavior was immoral in the real version of the story, you might very well think it's immoral in this version. But even if you think Shimp's behavior would be immoral in this version of the story, do you think that would make it okay for the state to force him to donate the bone marrow in this version? I doubt it. And if you don't think it would be okay for the state to do this, you should agree it should be legal for a woman to have an abortion not only regardless of how she got pregnant but regardless of why she doesn't want to remain pregnant. Since you should believe this because of what you believe about the different stories I've told about McFall and Shimp, and since McFall was a person with a right to life in each of those stories, you should believe that it should be legal for a woman to have an abortion in all these cases even if you believe every fetus is a person with a right to life, too. And since you think it would have been wrong for the state to force Shimp to let McFall use his bone marrow in these cases even if you think Shimp acted immorally by refusing to let McFall use it, you should agree that it should be legal for a woman to have an abortion in these cases even if you think it would be immoral for her to do so.

# 9

## Viability

A nervous young woman is pacing back and forth in the waiting room of a clinic in downtown Orlando. She came here to have an abortion. I've tried to convince you so far that it doesn't matter how she got pregnant or why she's unwilling to carry her pregnancy to term. Regardless of the circumstances that led her to walk into this clinic, the state shouldn't prevent her from carrying through with her plan. But one more thing might turn out to matter: how far along her pregnancy is. Does the view I've defended here mean abortion should be legal through all nine months of a woman's pregnancy?

Consider the case of Francine. Francine is nearly seven months pregnant. Until recently, she was thrilled about this. All the evidence showed she'd soon be delivering a healthy baby boy, and she'd already picked out a crib, changing table, baby clothes, and toys. She'd even settled on a name for her son: Frank. But a little over a week ago, Francine's boyfriend unexpectedly dumped her and headed out of town to be with another woman. Francine was devastated. After thinking about virtually nothing else since then, she's now decided she doesn't want to keep the baby. She wants nothing at all to do with her ex-boyfriend and she just can't picture herself raising a child on her own. Friends suggested she consider carrying the pregnancy to term and putting Frank up for adoption instead, but she can't stand the thought of having a child and then abandoning it to be raised by other people, either.

That's how she ended up in the waiting room of one of the few clinics in the country that performs late-term abortions.

Because Francine's pregnancy is so far along at this point, let's assume Frank is now viable. That means if Francine had a caesarean section today and Frank was removed from her body intact, Frank could survive outside her womb. He'd be born prematurely and he'd face some significant challenges at first, but let's assume for the sake of the example that he'd survive and ultimately be just fine. Should Francine be allowed to have an abortion at this late stage if that's the case?

This question makes many defenders of abortion rights particularly uncomfortable. They don't like the idea of defending abortion at such a late stage, but they don't see a good way to avoid defending it, either. The typical defense of abortion rights, after all, rests on the claim that the fetus isn't a person. Suppose Frank's lungs just became strong enough for him to survive outside the womb a few minutes ago. Ten minutes ago, he wasn't viable, but now he is. If typical defenders of abortion rights say Francine should have been allowed to abort Frank ten minutes ago but shouldn't be allowed to abort Frank now, they'd have to say that ten minutes ago Frank wasn't a person but now he is. And it's hard to see how just a little bit of extra lung development could make the difference between being a person and not being a person or between having a right to life and not having a right to life. As long as they rest their defense of abortion rights on the claim that the fetus isn't a person with a right to life before viability, then, defenders of abortion rights may well be stuck defending abortion rights after viability, too, whether they like it or not.

But the defense of abortion rights I've offered here doesn't depend on the claim that Frank isn't a person. Quite the opposite: I've been assuming all along, at least for the sake of the argument, that every human fetus is a person and that every human fetus has a right to life. And I've been trying to convince you that abortion should be legal even if this assumption is true. So what does my approach to defending abortion rights imply about the case of Francine? Yet again, the answer lies in changing the story of McFall and Shimp.

So suppose when Shimp learned McFall needed his bone marrow, he decided to go ahead and help his cousin out. He went down to the hospital, had himself connected to the bone marrow transferring machine, and patiently waited in his bed as the bone marrow slowly made its way from his body to McFall's. Suppose after a few hours, McFall received just enough bone marrow from Shimp to enable him to survive on his own and that Shimp then changed his mind and no longer wanted to help his cousin out. I assume you'll agree that it would be wrong for the state to prevent Shimp from being disconnected from the machine at this point, especially since McFall could now survive without Shimp's assistance. But suppose at this point Shimp decided he wanted more than just to be disconnected from the machine. Suppose he said this: "I don't just want to stop helping keep McFall alive. I want to make sure he ends up dead. I don't like the idea of having a cousin and so what I want is not simply to avoid the burden of keeping him alive. I want to kill him."

Nothing I've said here suggests the state should let Shimp kill McFall at this point. The lesson we're entitled to draw from the case of *McFall v. Shimp* is that Shimp should have the legal right to decide not to let McFall use his body even if McFall needs to use his body to stay alive. This doesn't mean Shimp should also have the right to kill McFall if McFall could survive without Shimp's assistance. In the same way, and for the same reason, my defense of the claim that a woman should have the legal right to decide not to let the fetus use her body when the fetus needs to use her body doesn't mean she should also have the legal right to kill the fetus when the fetus can survive without using her body. So the defense of abortion rights I've offered here doesn't mean abortion should be legal after the fetus is viable.

This doesn't mean abortion should be illegal after viability. There might be some other reason to think it should still be legal at that point. But if there is such a reason, you won't find it here. As far as this book is concerned, abortion should be legal at least up to the point of viability even if every fetus is a person, but perhaps legal only up to that point. Since the vast majority of abortions take place well before viability, this means abortion should be legal at least in the vast majority of cases, but perhaps not in all cases.

## 10

## Infanticide

Gloria is a new mom. Three months ago, she gave birth to a delightful baby girl named Gabriella. Everyone calls her Gabby. Most of the time, Gloria is excited about this blessed event. But once in a while, she wonders if she's made a big mistake. She's just 19, still hasn't finished high school, and is starting to realize how difficult all this is turning out to be.

I'm going to go out on a limb here and assume you think it would be wrong for Gloria to kill Gabby at this point. One of the most popular pro-life arguments starts with this assumption and goes something like this: A 3-month-old infant has a right to life. There's no difference between a 3-month-old infant and an infant one second short of being 3 months old that could make the 3-month-old infant have a right to life now but not have a right to life one second earlier. So if a 3-month-old infant has a right to life, so does an infant who's one second short of being 3 months old. But there's also no difference between an infant who's one second short of being 3 months old and an infant one second before then that could make the infant one second short of being 3 months old have a right to life but not have a right to life one second before then. So if an infant who's one second short of being 3 months old has a right to life, so does an infant who's two seconds short of being 3 months old. We can keep going back, second by second, as far as we want in the infant's life and we're never going to find a point where we think the infant has a right to life now but didn't have it one second earlier. And so we can keep repeating this argument over and over again until we get all the way back to the point when the infant was first conceived. So if we agree that a 3-month-old-infant has a right to life, we should also agree that the fetus has a right to life from the moment the fetus is conceived. And if it should be illegal for Gloria to kill Gabby when Gabby is 3 months old, it seems to follow that it should also be illegal for Gloria to have an abortion during any stage of Gabby's fetal development.

This kind of argument poses a potential problem for those who defend abortion rights by saying the fetus isn't a person. There are a variety of ways they can try to respond to this problem, but I'm not going to talk about them here. I'm not going to talk about them here because this kind of argument doesn't pose a problem for my defense of abortion rights in the first place. And it doesn't pose a problem for my defense of abortion rights because my defense of abortion rights doesn't depend on the claim that the fetus isn't a person. Making one more change to the story of McFall and Shimp can help make this clear.

So suppose again that when Shimp heard McFall needed his bone marrow, he went down to the hospital, had himself connected to the bone marrow transferring machine, and let McFall have all the bone marrow he needed. But now suppose three months after they both left the hospital feeling just fine, Shimp decided he'd made a big mistake. He now wishes he'd never let McFall use his body in the first place. He doesn't like having a cousin. He wants to kill him. Nothing I've said here suggests the state should let Shimp kill McFall at this point. Again, the lesson we're entitled to draw from the case of *McFall v. Shimp* is that Shimp should have the legal right to decide not to let McFall use his body even though McFall needs to use his body to stay alive, not that Shimp should have the right to kill McFall if McFall can survive without Shimp's assistance.

In the same way, and for the same reason, my defense of the claim that abortion should be legal even if the fetus is a person rests on the claim that a woman should have the legal right to decide not to let the fetus she's carrying use her body even though the fetus needs to use her body in order to stay alive. The claim that a woman should have the legal right to decide not to let the fetus use her body when the fetus needs to use her body doesn't mean she should also have the right to kill the fetus once the fetus can survive without using her body. For the same reason, it doesn't mean she should have the right to kill the fetus once it's developed into an adorable 3-month-old infant who is surviving outside her body. Or into a surly teenager, for that matter. So while some defenses of abortion rights might run the risk of committing their defenders to the claim that it should be legal to kill 3-month-old infants, the defense of abortion rights I've offered here doesn't.

# 11

## Feticide

Heather was a 26-year-old accountant who had recently moved to San Diego with her boyfriend when she found out she was pregnant. She'd been dating the guy for a while and they were starting to get serious. Heather was going to have a little boy and had already decided she wanted to name him Heath. She was really excited about it. But when she broke the news to her boyfriend, he said he wasn't ready to become a father. Heather was devastated and seriously considered having an abortion. But after thinking it over, she decided to carry the pregnancy to term. She hoped her boyfriend would come around. But if he didn't, she was prepared to raise Heath on her own.

Just a few weeks after she made her big decision, though, Heather was shot and killed in an attempted robbery. The robber could see that Heather was pregnant, but he shot her anyway. They eventually caught the guy who did it. And they didn't just charge him with one count of homicide. They charged him with two: one for killing Heather and one for killing Heath. That's because under California law, if you kill a pregnant woman and the fetus dies as a result, the fetus counts as a second homicide victim. Nearly forty states have laws like this. They're known as fetal homicide laws, or "feticide" laws for short. They differ in the details, but what they have in common is this: they identify a particular set of crimes that might be committed against a pregnant woman and they say if her fetus is killed or injured as a result of committing one of these crimes, or at least if it's killed or injured during a certain specified stage of fetal development, then the fetus can be treated as a victim of the crime, too. And it doesn't matter if the pregnant woman survives the attack. Even if Heather had pulled through the surgery after she was shot, the shooter still could have been charged with homicide for killing Heath. There's a federal law like this, too. The Unborn Victims of Violence Act of 2004 lists over sixty federal crimes and says the woman's fetus counts as a legal victim if the fetus is injured or killed during the commission of any of them.

People who are pro-life sometimes point to these feticide laws and complain that there's a double standard here. If Heather wants to carry her pregnancy to term and an armed robber kills Heath, the law says killing Heath is murder. If Heather wants to have an abortion and the abortion kills Heath, the law says killing Heath isn't murder. It's almost as if whether Heath is a person, or whether Heath has a right to life, somehow depends on whether Heather wants to have him. And that's absurd. So if it's murder when the armed robber kills Heath, these pro-life people say, it should be murder when Heather has an abortion, too. And if it's murder when Heather has an abortion, then it should be illegal for Heather to have an abortion.

Many people who are pro-choice seem to come to a similar conclusion about feticide laws, but from the opposite direction. They think abortion should be legal because they think the fetus isn't a person and they object to feticide laws precisely because such laws treat the fetus as if it is a person. They think it should be legal for Heather to have an abortion and because of this they think Heath shouldn't be counted as a second victim when a crime is committed against Heather. So there's something a lot of people on both sides of the abortion debate seem to agree about here: feticide laws and laws against abortion should stand or fall together. Pro-life people who think this think the two kinds of law should stand together while pro-choice people who think this think the two kinds of law should fall together, but they both think there's some kind of inconsistency or double standard involved in having one kind of law without the other.

I think people on both sides of the abortion debate who hold this view are mistaken. There's nothing inconsistent about saying abortion should be legal and also saying the fetus should count as a second victim in cases like that of Heather and Heath. And once again, I think the case of McFall and Shimp can help us see this. So suppose Shimp decided he was willing to let McFall have some of his bone marrow. He walked down to the hospital and connected himself to the bone marrow transferring machine and the machine slowly started removing some of his bone marrow and giving it to McFall. And suppose before McFall received enough of Shimp's bone marrow to survive, an armed robber shot and killed Shimp, knowing full well that by killing Shimp he would also be depriving McFall of the bone marrow supply he needed.

In this version of the story, killing Shimp also means killing McFall by depriving McFall of the bone marrow Shimp was giving him. So it wouldn't be particularly unreasonable if the state decided to charge the robber with two counts of homicide: one for killing Shimp by shooting him and one for killing McFall by cutting off his supply of bone marrow. But nothing about treating the case this way suggests it would be okay for the state to force Shimp to let McFall have the bone marrow if Shimp decided not to let McFall have it. Saying Shimp should have the right not to let McFall use his bone marrow if he doesn't want to let him use it doesn't mean other people should have the right to prevent McFall from receiving Shimp's bone marrow if Shimp decides he does want to let McFall use it. And when the robber killed Shimp, he prevented McFall from receiving the bone marrow Shimp was giving him. So it's perfectly consistent to say the state should allow Shimp to decide whether to let McFall use his bone marrow while also saying the state should treat McFall as a second victim if an armed robber kills both of them. Shimp has the right to deprive McFall of the use of his bone marrow because it's Shimp's bone marrow and Shimp has the right to decide what to do with it. That doesn't mean an armed robber has the right to deprive McFall of Shimp's bone marrow because Shimp's bone marrow doesn't belong to the armed robber. I'm pretty sure you'll agree with me about this regardless of whether you see yourself as pro-life, pro-choice, or somewhere in between.

But if I'm right about that, you should say the same thing about feticide laws and laws against abortion, whether you're pro-life, pro-choice, or somewhere in between. There's nothing inconsistent about saying Heather should have the right not to let Heath use her uterus if she doesn't want to let him use it and also saying other people shouldn't have the right to prevent Heath from using Heather's uterus if she does want to let him use it. And when the robber killed Heather, he prevented Heath from using Heather's uterus. He had no right to do this. When the robber killed Heather, he also killed Heath by depriving him of the life support Heather was giving him, just as when the robber killed Shimp, he also killed McFall by depriving him of the bone marrow Shimp was giving him.

Saying there were two victims in the case of McFall and Shimp doesn't mean it would have been okay for the state to force Shimp to let McFall use his bone marrow if he didn't want to let him use it. In the same way, and for the same reason, saying there were two victims in the case of Heather and Heath doesn't mean it would have been okay for the state to force Heather to let Heath use her uterus if she didn't want to let him use it. Heather has the right to deprive Heath of the use of her uterus because it's Heather's uterus and Heather has the right to decide what to do with it. That doesn't mean an armed robber has the right to deprive Heath of the use of Heather's uterus because Heather's uterus doesn't belong to the armed robber. Again, there's nothing inconsistent about saying these two things—no hypocrisy or double standard. If anything, there's clearly a single standard operating in both cases: Shimp and only Shimp gets to decide whether to let McFall use his bone marrow, and Heather and only Heather gets to decide whether to let Heath use her uterus.

Some defenses of abortion rights depend on the claim that the fetus isn't a person. Those defenses of abortion rights do seem to commit their defenders to opposing feticide laws. But the defense of abortion rights I'm offering in this book doesn't depend on the claim that the fetus isn't a person. So accepting my defense of abortion rights doesn't commit you to opposing feticide laws. What accepting my defense of abortion rights does commit you to is accepting that abortion should be legal at least up to the point where the fetus is viable. I've tried to convince you to accept this if you think Judge Flaherty made the right call in *McFall v. Shimp*, even if you think every fetus is a person with a right to life and even if you think abortion is immoral. And I've tried to explain why nothing I said to convince you of this means abortion should be legal after the fetus is viable, or that it should be legal to kill infants or teenagers, or that it should be legal to kill or injure the fetus of a woman who's decided to carry her pregnancy to term. I'm now finished explaining what my position is, and what it isn't, and offering it an initial defense. You probably have some objections at this point. Let's move on to them.

# PART II

# OBJECTIONS AND RESPONSES

# 12

## Consent

Some objections to the argument I presented in part I try to show that the lesson of *McFall v. Shimp* can't be used to justify abortion rights even in cases of rape. But I want to start with an objection that allows, at least for the sake of the argument, that my argument might work in rape cases, and that tries to show that even if it does, it still fails in every other case. This objection is based on the idea that there's an important difference between situations that are caused by a voluntary act and situations that aren't. And it claims that because of this difference, a fetus conceived during sex that's voluntary has a right to use the pregnant woman's body even if a fetus conceived as a result of rape doesn't.

There are a few reasons to begin with this objection. First, it's the most common objection to the kind of argument I defended in part I. So it's one you're most likely thinking of already. Second, the basic claim the objection depends on—the claim that there's an important difference between situations that are caused by a voluntary act and situations that aren't—seems hard to deny. So this objection seems particularly promising. Finally, most pregnancies are not the result of rape. So if this objection is successful, it means my defense of abortion rights won't work in most cases even if it can overcome every other objection that can be raised against it. As a result, I'd better have a good response to this objection.

I think I do have a good response. But what the response is depends on what, exactly, the objection is. And what, exactly, the objection is depends on why we're supposed to think the difference between situations that are caused by voluntary acts and situations that aren't matters in the first place. One reason to think this difference matters has to do with the relationship between doing a voluntary act and giving valid consent to something. Suppose a robber points a gun at you and says "Give me your money or I'll shoot you in the head." If you give the robber your money, it's not plausible to say you gave valid consent to let him keep it. And it's not plausible to say you gave valid consent to let him keep it because it's not plausible to say you gave it to him voluntarily. He forced you to give him the money. But suppose a car salesman points a car out to you and says "Give me your money and I'll let you drive this car home today." If you give the car salesman your money, it is plausible to say you gave valid consent to let him keep it. And it's plausible to say you gave valid consent to let him keep it because it's plausible to say you gave it to him voluntarily. He didn't force you to give him the money. You freely chose to give it to him.

In these two cases, at least, the difference between doing a voluntary act and not doing a voluntary act seems to matter because it seems to make the difference between giving valid consent to something and not giving valid consent. This suggests one way the difference between situations that are caused by voluntary acts and situations that aren't might be used to show that my defense of abortion rights only works, if it works at all, in cases involving rape. When a woman is raped, the critic can say, she doesn't do a voluntary act that leads to the situation where the fetus is using her body and so she can't reasonably be taken to have given valid consent to let the fetus use her body. But when a woman's pregnancy is the result of her freely choosing to have sex, the critic can add, her voluntary act of having sex can reasonably count as her giving valid consent to accept the consequences of her act. If this view is correct, then while Al doesn't have the right to use Alice's body because Alice was raped, Bob does have the right to use Barbara's body because Barbara had sex voluntarily. This would mean that while it might be wrong for the state to prevent Alice from having an abortion, it would not be wrong for the state to prevent Barbara from having one. And the same would go for Carol, Dorothy, Elaine, and any other woman who got pregnant as a result of freely choosing to have sex with someone.

There are, of course, differences between the case where you voluntarily give your money to a car salesman and the case where Barbara voluntarily has sex with the guy she met at the party. For one thing, in the car salesman case, you give explicit consent to letting the salesman have your money. You sign a document that specifically says you're agreeing to pay the amount shown on the bill. But when Barbara freely chose to have sex with that guy, she didn't explicitly consent to let the fetus use her body for nine months if she got pregnant as a result. She didn't sign a document saying she agreed not to have an abortion if she got pregnant. This is an important difference between the two cases. It shows that just because we agree you've given valid consent to let the car salesman have your money, it doesn't mean we have to agree Barbara has given valid consent to let Bob use her body. We could say you've given valid consent to let the car salesman have your money because you explicitly agreed to let him have it. This wouldn't commit us to saying Barbara has given valid consent to let Bob use her body because Barbara didn't explicitly agree to let Bob use her body. But this difference between the two cases doesn't show that an objection based on the connection between voluntary acts and valid consent can't undermine the defense of abortion rights I've offered here. It just shows that if it's going to succeed, the objection will have to be based on a different kind of example. And this by itself isn't a problem for the critic because there are other cases where it does seem like someone has given valid consent to something even though they never explicitly said they were consenting to it.

Suppose you sit down at a restaurant, for example, and when the server asks what you'd like for dinner, you say "I'd like the lasagna." When you tell the server you'd like the lasagna, you don't explicitly add "and I hereby agree to pay for it." You don't sign a contract explicitly agreeing you'll pay for it, either. Still, it seems fair to say by telling the server you'd like the lasagna, you've agreed to pay for it. You haven't explicitly consented to this. But you've consented to it anyway. You've consented tacitly. Or suppose you leave some money on the table as a tip after you've paid the bill. You don't explicitly say "I hereby agree to let the server have this money." You don't sign a contract to that effect, either. But it seems fair to say you've tacitly consented to let the server have the money anyway. And if you put some of your chips down on red at a casino's roulette table, you don't explicitly say "the casino can keep these chips if the ball lands on black" or sign a contract to that effect, either. But, again, it seems fair to say you've tacitly consented to let the casino keep the chips if the ball lands on black all the same. Cases like this might be used to try to show that by freely choosing to have sex, Barbara tacitly consented to let Bob use her body even if she didn't explicitly consent to let him use it.

The case where you put some of your chips on red at the roulette table seems to be the most promising example for the critic. When you freely put your chips on red, you knowingly take a gamble. You hope things will turn out well for you and that the ball will land on red, but you realize they might not. And if the ball lands on black, you have no one to blame but yourself. You took a gamble and lost, and now you have to accept the consequences. Similarly, the critic might say, when Barbara freely chose to have sex with the guy she met at the party, she knowingly took a gamble. She hoped things would turn out well for her and that she wouldn't get pregnant, but she realized she might get pregnant all the same. And she knew if she did get pregnant, she'd have no one to blame but herself. Barbara took a gamble and lost, and now she, too, has to accept the consequences. If we agree you've given valid consent to let the casino keep your chips when you gamble on the roulette wheel and lose, the critic can say, we have to agree Barbara gave valid consent to let Bob her use her body when she gambled on sex and lost. And if Barbara really has given valid consent to let Bob use her body, the critic seems entitled to conclude that there's nothing wrong with the state protecting that right by preventing her from having an abortion. This seems like the strongest version of the objection based on the relationship between doing a voluntary act and validly consenting to something. I'll call it the *consent objection*.

The consent objection might look like a good objection to my argument. But I don't think it is. The problem has to do with a difference between the case of you and the roulette wheel and the case of Barbara and the guy she met at the party. In the case of you and the roulette wheel, there's a widely recognized social convention operating in the background. The convention says when you put your chips down on red at the table, you by that very act communicate your agreement to let the casino keep them if the ball lands on black. It's only because of this widely recognized social convention that it makes sense to say your act counts as the act of consenting to let the casino keep the chips if the ball lands on black. I think you'll agree with this claim if you imagine a case where someone does the very same act in a society where there's no such convention. Picture a casino in a society where if you want to place a bet on red, you have to sign a piece of paper that says you're betting on red and that specifies the amount you're betting. There's no other way in this society to communicate your bet to the casino. In this society, you can put your chips down anywhere you want. They're yours to keep unless you lose them, and you can only lose them by signing a betting form and losing the bet. Now suppose in this society someone puts some of their chips down on the red part of the table because their pockets are getting too full, and suppose the ball then lands on black. Do you think they've agreed to let the casino keep the chips in this case? I doubt it. I think you'll find it clear that they haven't agreed to let the casino keep the chips in this case. And I think you'll find it clear precisely because in this society there's no social convention by which putting your chips down on red means you're betting on red.

The same goes for the other cases I pointed to as examples where it's plausible to think someone has consented to something even though they haven't explicitly consented to it. When you tell the server you'd like the lasagna, for example, you tacitly agree that you'll pay for it even though you don't explicitly agree to pay for it. But imagine a society where all restaurants are run by the government and where the government pays for all the food. In that case, if a server asks what you want for dinner and you say you'd like some lasagna, do you think you've tacitly agreed to pay for it? I doubt it. Or picture a society where no one has ever left a tip for a server. In that society, there would be no reason to think leaving some money on the table after a meal meant you'd agreed to give it to the server. How would anyone know to interpret your act that way?

This lesson holds in any case where it's reasonable to interpret someone's act as tacitly consenting to something. In this society, if you get in a taxi and tell the driver where you want to go, you're tacitly agreeing to pay for the ride when you get there. If you raise your hand at an auction, you're tacitly agreeing to pay the named price for the item on sale. But if you get in a taxi in a country where taxis are free, or raise your hand at an auction in a society where only written bids are accepted at auctions, then you haven't tacitly agreed to these things. Your voluntary act can count as tacitly consenting to do something, then, only if it takes place in a social context where doing the act is widely recognized as a way of intentionally communicating your agreement to do it. I'm pretty sure you'll have the same reaction I have to the cases I've discussed here. And if you do have the same reaction I have, you'll have to agree that tacit consent requires the existence of a social convention in this way.

With this lesson in mind, let's now return to the case of Barbara and the guy she met at the party. Barbara's voluntary act was the act of having sex with this guy. Is it reasonable to view this act as Barbara's tacitly consenting to carry her pregnancy to term if the birth control fails? I don't see how it can be if tacit consent requires a social convention in the way we've just seen it does. Putting your chips on red, at least in this society, means "I'm placing a bet on red." It's a convention we've come up with so you can communicate your bet without having to say so explicitly. Raising your hand at an auction, at least in many contexts, means "I agree to pay the amount currently being asked." It's a convention that allows you to communicate your agreement without having to say anything. We have a convention on which leaving money on the table after a meal is understood by all involved to mean it's a tip for the server. The convention lets you communicate your agreement to let the server have the money without having to say so explicitly. And so on. But having sex is clearly not a convention we've come up with to allow women to indicate, without having to say so explicitly, that they agree to give a fetus the right to remain in their uterus. Having sex simply isn't a means of communication in the way that raising your hand or leaving money or chips on a table is. People put chips on red in order to let the croupier know they're agreeing to let the house keep the money if the ball lands on black. Women don't have sex with men in order to let the men know that they're agreeing to let a fetus use their uterus if they end up getting pregnant. The consent objection claims that because Barbara's act was voluntary and because she knew she might get pregnant as a result of it, her act counts as tacitly consenting to give Bob the right to use her body. But if you agree that a voluntary act can count as tacitly consenting to something only if there's a widely recognized social convention on which the act counts as a way of deliberately communicating that consent, then you'll have to deny this claim. There's clearly no such convention in the case of Barbara's act. So you can't interpret Barbara as agreeing to let Bob use her body just because she agreed to have sex with the guy she met at the party.

I think that's a good reason to reject the consent objection. But suppose you're not convinced. I think a voluntary act can count as tacitly consenting to something only if there's a widely recognized social convention on which people choose to do the act in order to express their agreement to do whatever that something is. But suppose you think the existence of such a convention isn't necessary for tacit consent. You think as long as an act is voluntary and is done knowing it might produce a certain result, the person who does the act tacitly gives valid consent to accepting that result. If you think this, you'll think Barbara has given valid consent to let Bob use her uterus because Barbara had sex with the guy she met at the party voluntarily and she knew that having sex with the guy might result in her getting pregnant. But if you think this, your thinking will have implications in other cases that I doubt you'll be willing to accept. And if I'm right about that, this provides a second reason for you to reject the consent objection.

So go back to one of my fictional versions of the story of McFall and Shimp, the one where Shimp goes to visit McFall in the hospital, slips and falls on the recently polished floor, and ends up stuck to the bone marrow transferring machine. Shimp freely chose to walk across the slippery floor and he did it knowing that if he did, it might result in his becoming stuck to the bone marrow transferring machine. If all that's needed for an act to count as giving valid consent to accepting a situation is that the act is voluntary and the person doing the act knows the act might lead to that situation, then Shimp has given valid consent to stay plugged into the bone marrow transferring machine. But if you were in Shimp's shoes, as it were, and if you had slipped on the floor as you walked across the room, I doubt you'd agree that simply by walking across the room you had somehow agreed to let McFall have the bone marrow he needed if you slipped and fell onto the machine. And if you don't think you would have given valid consent to letting McFall use your bone marrow in this case, then you can't think Barbara gave valid consent to letting Bob use her uterus simply because she had sex voluntarily and knew the act might lead to a situation where Bob was using her uterus.

Or consider a more straightforward version of the story. Suppose after learning of his cousin's predicament, Shimp walked straight to the hospital, sat down next to McFall, and freely chose to plug himself into the bone marrow transferring machine. In this version of the story, it's even clearer that Shimp did a voluntary act knowing the result might be that he'd end up being plugged into the bone marrow transferring machine because in this case, his voluntary act just is the act of being plugged into the machine. But even in this version of the story, I doubt you'll think that just because he did this act voluntarily, he's given valid consent to stay plugged into the machine until McFall has gotten all the bone marrow he needs. Does the fact that you voluntarily start to help someone mean you automatically agree to continue helping them for as long as they need your help? I doubt you'll think so. And if

I'm right, then you'll have to agree that Shimp hasn't given valid consent to let McFall continue using his body in this case, too. But if you agree Shimp hasn't given valid consent to let McFall continue using his body in this case, then you'll again have to agree that the mere fact that a person does an act voluntarily knowing it might produce a certain result isn't enough to show they've given valid consent to accepting that result. And if you agree with that, then, again, you can't say Barbara has given valid consent to let Bob use her uterus just because she freely and voluntarily had sex with the guy she met at the party and knew that having sex with the guy might result in Bob's starting to use her uterus. This gives you a second reason to reject the consent objection.

# 13

# Responsibility

The consent objection tries to show that the difference between situations that are caused by a voluntary act and situations that aren't undermines my argument. I've tried to convince you not to accept this objection. But the consent objection isn't the only way to try to show that this difference undermines my argument. A second way to try to show this appeals to a claim about responsibility. The claim is this: If you do a voluntary act that causes someone to need your assistance, then you're responsible for providing them with that assistance. When I say your act causes someone to need your assistance, I mean if you hadn't done the act they wouldn't need your assistance, and given that you did do the act, they do need your assistance. When I say they need your assistance, I mean you're the only person who can help them and if you don't help them, they'll die. When I say you're responsible for providing them with that assistance, I mean they have a right to your assistance, not that it would simply be nice of you to provide it. They have a right to your assistance precisely because you're the one who caused them to need it. And in saying all this, I'm assuming when you did the act in question, you knew there was a chance it would cause someone to need your assistance in this way. So another way to put the claim about responsibility is this: if as a foreseeable result of your voluntary act someone will die if you don't assist them, and if they wouldn't need your assistance if you hadn't done the act, then they have a right to your assistance. I'll call this the *responsibility principle*.

My guess is the responsibility principle will strike you as pretty plausible. If it's your fault someone needs your help, you'll probably agree it's only fair to say you have to help them. And the implications of the responsibility principle will probably strike you as pretty plausible, too. Suppose Todd decides to go hunting in the woods one day just for the fun of it. He knows when people go hunting they sometimes accidentally shoot innocent bystanders, and he takes every reasonable precaution to avoid having this happen short of not going hunting at all. Unfortunately, one of Todd's bullets ends up striking little Timmy, a young child who was playing in his backyard just beyond the woods. Little Timmy is now bleeding to death. Emergency medics arrive on the scene and quickly determine that Timmy's blood type is B-negative. They don't have any suitable blood on hand for Timmy, but it turns out Todd's blood type is B-negative, too. So they tell Todd to roll up his sleeve.

Now suppose Todd says something like this: "Hey, wait a minute! I didn't shoot that kid on purpose. I was really careful. It was just an accident. You know, these things happen. It's my body, and my blood, and so it's my right to choose, and I really hate the way it feels when they prick your skin with a needle. Plus, giving blood makes me nauseous. I tried it one time and it was awful. It's too bad the kid's in this situation, but I never promised I'd help out if I accidentally shot anyone, so it's not like he has the right to my blood or anything. So, no, I'm not going to roll up my sleeve." Do you think Todd's response here is reasonable? You probably don't. You probably think it doesn't matter that Todd didn't shoot little Timmy on purpose. You probably think it doesn't matter that Todd took reasonable precautions to try to avoid shooting him. And you probably think it doesn't matter that Todd never gave tacit or explicit consent to help someone if he ended up accidentally shooting them. What you probably think is the fact that Todd knew he might cause something like this to happen when he went hunting is enough by itself to make him responsible for giving some of his blood to Timmy now. And if you think this, then you agree with the responsibility principle: Timmy has the right to some of Todd's blood because it's Todd's fault Timmy needs the blood.

I'm going to assume you agree with the responsibility principle. If you do agree with it, here's how you can use it to generate a problem for my argument. First, take the principle and apply it to the cases of Alice and Barbara. Al needs to use Alice's body to go on living. Did Alice do a voluntary act that caused Al to be in this needy condition? No, she didn't. Alice was raped while she was unconscious. So the responsibility principle doesn't apply to her. What about Barbara? Bob needs to use Barbara's body to go on living. Did Barbara do a voluntary act that caused Bob to be in this needy condition? Remember, when I say your act causes someone to need your assistance, I mean if you hadn't done the act, they wouldn't need your assistance, and given that you did do the act, they do need your assistance. Barbara freely chose to have sex with the guy she met at the party. If she hadn't had sex with the guy, Bob wouldn't need to use her body because she wouldn't be pregnant. Given that she did have sex with the guy, Bob does need to use her body because Bob's a fetus and that's what fetuses need in order to go on living.

So, yes, Barbara did do a voluntary act that caused Bob to need her assistance. Because she had sex with the guy she met at the party, Bob needs to use her body in order to go on living. If the responsibility principle is true, this means Bob has the right to use her body. He didn't get that right because Barbara consented to give it to him. But he got that right all the same. He got the right to use Barbara's body because Barbara is responsible for the fact that he now needs to use her body. If the responsibility principle is true, then, even though Al doesn't have the right to use Alice's body, Bob does have the right to use Barbara's body. And the fetus will also have the right to use the woman's body in the case of Carol, Dorothy, Elaine, and any other woman who gets pregnant by choosing to have sex with someone. The case for abortion rights I've offered here will turn out to work, if it works at all, only in cases involving rape. That's a big problem for my position.

And there's an even bigger problem. Remember how I tried to convince you it should be legal for Barbara to have an abortion? I gave you a version of the story of McFall and Shimp where Shimp walked across the slippery floor even though he knew this might lead him to slip and fall and get stuck to the bone marrow transferring machine. And I said if you agree this doesn't mean McFall has the right to continue using Shimp's body in this version of the story, you should agree that the fact that Barbara knew she might get pregnant if she had sex with the guy she met at the party doesn't mean Bob now has the right to continue using her body, either. In the context of the consent objection, that was a fair comparison. If what Shimp did isn't enough to count as consenting to let McFall use his body, then what Barbara did isn't enough to count as consenting to let Bob use her body.

But if the responsibility principle is true, there's still a big difference between these cases. That's because Barbara is responsible for the fact that Bob needs to use her body. He needs to use her body because of what Barbara did. But Shimp isn't responsible for the fact that McFall needs to use his body. McFall needs to use Shimp's body because McFall has aplastic anemia, and Shimp didn't do anything to cause McFall to have aplastic anemia. So not only is there an important difference between the case of Alice and the case of Barbara, but there's also an important difference between the case of Barbara and the version of the story of McFall and Shimp I compared to the case of

Barbara. Even if you agree Shimp should have the right not to keep McFall alive in that version of the story, then, this doesn't show you should agree Barbara should have the right not to keep Bob alive after all. You can say Shimp doesn't have to help McFall because Shimp isn't responsible for the fact that McFall needs his help. And if that's why you think Shimp doesn't have to help McFall, this won't support my claim that Barbara doesn't have to help Bob. It won't support that claim because Barbara really is responsible for the fact that Bob needs her help. And that's an even bigger problem for my position.

And there's an even bigger problem than this. Because if I change the story of McFall and Shimp and try to make it more like the case of Bob and Barbara in terms of responsibility, you'll probably think the change in the story really does make a difference. Suppose the story went like this: Robert McFall was perfectly healthy. David Shimp wanted to set off some fireworks near McFall's house. Shimp knew the fireworks contained toxic chemicals, knew that if he set them off near McFall's house there was a chance McFall would be exposed to them, and knew if McFall was exposed to them, this might cause McFall to develop aplastic anemia. Shimp decided to set the fireworks off near McFall's house anyway, just for the fun of it. He took every reasonable precaution he could to prevent McFall from being exposed to the toxic chemicals short of not setting them off at all. Unfortunately, McFall was exposed to the toxic chemicals and that's why he has aplastic anemia and now needs Shimp's bone marrow in order to survive.

Now suppose in this version of the story Shimp once again declares he's unwilling to let McFall have any of his bone marrow. Your reaction to Shimp's situation is probably going to be different this time. You'll probably think McFall really does have a right to use some of Shimp's bone marrow in this version of the story. And you'll probably think this precisely because it's

Shimp's fault that McFall needs it in this version of the story. That, at least, is what you'll think if you agree with the responsibility principle. After all, the responsibility principle says if you do a voluntary act that causes someone to need your assistance, then you're responsible for providing them with that assistance. And I think you'll agree with the responsibility principle.

If I'm right about this, then not only does the responsibility principle mean my original argument fails to show it should be legal for Barbara to have an abortion, but when I try to fix the argument by changing the story of McFall and Shimp to make it more like the case of Bob and Barbara, it actually shows that Bob really does have the right to use Barbara's body and that Barbara really shouldn't be allowed to have an abortion. In short, you probably think the responsibility principle is true, and if you do, it seems to show you should think my claim that Barbara should be allowed to have an abortion is not just unsupported but also positively false. And the same would go for my claims about Carol, Dorothy, Elaine, and any other woman who gets pregnant by choosing to have sex with someone. That's a really big problem. I'll call the objection that raises this problem the *responsibility objection*.

I think the responsibility objection is stronger than the consent objection. But I don't think it's strong enough. The reason for this is a bit complicated. It has to do with an ambiguity in something I said before about what it means for your act to cause someone to need your assistance. Because of this ambiguity, there's an ambiguity about just what, exactly, the responsibility principle says. The responsibility objection depends on the responsibility principle. So we can't figure out whether the responsibility objection is a good objection until we get more clear about just what, exactly, the responsibility principle says. And I think once we get clearer about this, we'll see that while the responsibility objection is a good objection, it isn't good enough.

So let's go back to my earlier clarification that when I say your act causes someone to need your assistance, I mean if you hadn't done the act, they wouldn't need your assistance and given that you did do the act, they do need your assistance. It turns out this clarification wasn't clear enough. That's because there's two ways you can do an act that results in someone needing your assistance and have it turn out that if you hadn't done the act, the person wouldn't need your assistance. Here's one way that can happen. Suppose if you hadn't done what you did, this other person wouldn't exist. If this other person wouldn't exist, they wouldn't need your assistance. In order for a person to need your assistance, after all, that person has to exist. So one way you can cause someone to need your assistance is to do an act such that they now need your assistance and if you hadn't done the act they wouldn't exist now and so wouldn't need your assistance.

But here's a second and very different way you can cause someone to need your assistance. Suppose if you hadn't done what you did this other person would exist now and they'd be able to get along just fine without you. If this other person would be able to get along just fine without you, then they wouldn't need your assistance. They wouldn't need your assistance not because they wouldn't exist but because they would exist and would be doing just fine without your help. So a second way you can cause someone to need your assistance is to do an act such that they now need your assistance and if you hadn't done the act they would now exist and would be able to get along just fine without you.

In both of these cases, you cause it to be true that another person now needs your assistance. But you cause it to be true in very different ways. In the first case, you cause it to be true that another person now needs your assistance by causing a needy person to exist now. If you hadn't done what you did, the needy person wouldn't exist now. In the second kind of case, you cause it to be true that another person now needs your assistance by causing an existing person to be needy. If you hadn't done what you did, the existing person would exist now, but they wouldn't be needy now. We might say in the first case, you cause the existence of a needy person and in the second case, you cause the neediness of an already existing person.

The responsibility principle says if you do a voluntary act that causes someone to need your assistance, then you're responsible for providing them with that assistance. Since my original clarification about what it means to cause someone to need your assistance was ambiguous, it turns out my original presentation of the responsibility principle was ambiguous, too. It could mean you're responsible for providing someone with assistance if you do a voluntary act that causes them to need your assistance in the first sense. Or it could mean you're responsible for providing someone with assistance if you do a voluntary act that causes them to need your assistance in the second sense. And that means there's not just one responsibility principle. There are two.

The first responsibility principle says this: if it's true that if you hadn't done what you did, the needy person wouldn't exist now, then you're responsible for providing them with the assistance they need. The second responsibility principle says this: if it's true that if you hadn't done what you did, the needy person would exist now and wouldn't be needy, then you're responsible for providing them with the assistance they need. The first principle says if you cause a needy person to exist rather than to not exist, then you're responsible for providing them with the assistance they need. The second principle says if you cause an already existing person to be needy rather than to not be needy, then you're responsible for providing them with the assistance they need.

Now that we've seen how my original presentation of the responsibility principle was ambiguous, we can see that the responsibility objection is party right and partly wrong. I said the case of Bob and Barbara is like the version of the story of McFall and Shimp where Shimp slips and falls and gets stuck to the bone marrow transferring machine. Barbara and Shimp each do a voluntary act knowing there's a risk they'll end up stuck with someone else using their body to keep them alive. And I said if you think it would be wrong for the state to force Shimp to keep McFall alive in that version of the story, you should think it would be wrong for the state to force Barbara to keep Bob alive, too. The responsibility objection says I was wrong about this because Barbara is responsible for the fact that Bob needs her assistance in a way that Shimp isn't responsible for the fact that McFall needs his assistance.

Now that we have a clear understanding that there are two distinct responsibility principles, we can see that the responsibility objection is right about this. In the version of the story where Shimp slips on the floor and gets attached to the bone marrow transferring machine, Shimp isn't responsible for the fact that McFall needs his bone marrow in either of the two senses. It's not true that if Shimp hadn't walked across the floor McFall wouldn't exist now. McFall would exist either way. So the first responsibility principle doesn't apply to Shimp. And it's not true that if Shimp hadn't walked across the floor McFall would exist now and would be able to get along just fine without Shimp's bone marrow. McFall would have aplastic anemia either way. So the second responsibility principle doesn't apply to Shimp, either.

But Barbara is responsible for the fact that Bob now needs to use her body in the first sense, even though she isn't responsible for this fact in the second sense. It's not true that if Barbara hadn't had sex with the guy she met at the party Bob would exist now and would be able to get along just fine without her assistance. So the second responsibility principle doesn't apply to Barbara. But it is true that if Barbara hadn't had sex with the guy she met at the party Bob wouldn't exist now. If she hadn't had sex with the guy, Bob would never have been conceived. And if Bob had never been conceived, he wouldn't exist now. So the first responsibility principle does apply to Barbara while it doesn't apply to Shimp. Barbara is responsible for the fact that Bob needs her help in a way that Shimp isn't responsible for the fact that McFall needs Shimp's help. As a result of this difference, the responsibility objection is correct when it says you can't move directly from the claim that it would be wrong for the state to force Shimp to keep McFall alive to the conclusion that it would be wrong for the state to force Barbara to keep Bob alive. In this sense, the responsibility objection is right and I was wrong.

The responsibility objection then went on to claim that the case of Barbara is really like the version of the story of McFall and Shimp where Shimp sets off the toxic fireworks near McFall's house knowing if he does so, this might cause McFall to develop aplastic anemia. In both cases, the objection pointed out, one person's voluntary act causes another person to need their assistance. If we think McFall has the right to use some of Shimp's bone marrow in this version of the story, the objection said, we have to agree that Bob has the right to use Barbara's body. But now that we've gotten clear about the ambiguity in my initial presentation of the responsibility principle, we can see that this claim made by the responsibility objection is mistaken.

It's true that Shimp and Barbara each did an act that caused another person to need their assistance. But it's true in importantly different ways. If Shimp hadn't set off the fireworks near McFall's house, then McFall would now exist and would be able to get along just fine without Shimp's bone marrow. That's because McFall would now exist and wouldn't have aplastic anemia. This means the second responsibility principle applies to this version of the story of McFall and Shimp. The second principle says if it's true that if you hadn't done what you did, the needy person would exist now and would be able to get along just fine without you, then you're responsible for providing them with the assistance they need. So if we accept the second responsibility principle, we have to agree that McFall now has the right to use some of Shimp's bone marrow.

But the second responsibility principle doesn't apply to the case of Bob and Barbara. It's not true that if Barbara hadn't had sex with the guy she met at the party Bob would now exist and would be able to get along just fine without using her body. That's not true because if Barbara hadn't had sex with the guy she met at the party Bob wouldn't exist at all. So the second responsibility principle doesn't apply to Barbara while it does apply to the story of McFall and Shimp and the fireworks. But the first responsibility principle does apply to Barbara. The first responsibility principle says if it's true that if you hadn't done what you did, the needy person wouldn't exist now, then you're responsible for providing them with the assistance they need. So if we accept the first responsibility principle, we have to agree that Bob has the right to use Barbara's body.

Here's why the difference between the first responsibility principle and the second responsibility principle turns out to be so important. The story where Shimp sets off the fireworks is like the case where Todd goes hunting. Todd injured Timmy so he owes it to Timmy to help him recover from his injury. Shimp made McFall sick so he owes it to McFall to help him recover from his sickness. These are cases that involve the second responsibility principle. They're cases where one person does an act that causes a second person to go from a healthy condition to a needy condition. That's why they're cases where if the first person hadn't done the act in question, the second person would now exist and be able to get along just fine without the first person's help. But for the same reason, they're cases where the first person did an act that harmed the second person. And that's why it seems so hard to deny that the second person now has a right to the first person's assistance. The second responsibility principle seems so plausible, that is, because it rests on a principle of compensation that seems so plausible: if you harm someone, you have a responsibility to fix the harm and so the person you harmed has a right to your assistance. That's why it seems so clear that Todd owes some blood to Timmy after he accidentally shoots him and Shimp owes some bone marrow to McFall after he causes McFall to come down with aplastic anemia.

But cases involving the first responsibility principle are fundamentally different in this respect. They aren't cases where the first person has harmed the second person. Todd harmed Timmy by shooting him, and Shimp harmed McFall by causing him to contract aplastic anemia, but Barbara didn't harm Bob by conceiving him. Timmy would have been better off if Todd hadn't shot him, and McFall would have been better off if Shimp hadn't set off the fireworks near his house, but Bob wouldn't have been better off if Barbara hadn't conceived him. Bob wouldn't have existed at all. So the reason Shimp would owe McFall some bone marrow in the version of the story where he made McFall sick doesn't apply to the case where Barbara causes Bob to need to use her uterus by having sex with the guy she met at the party. As a result, the responsibility objection is wrong when it says if we think McFall has the right to use some of Shimp's bone marrow in that version of the story then we have to think Bob has the right to use Barbara's uterus. McFall has the right to some of Shimp's bone marrow because Shimp harmed him and now owes him compensation. That doesn't show that Bob has the right to use Barbara's uterus because Barbara didn't harm Bob and so she doesn't owe him compensation.

So what have we learned so far? We've figured out what the question is and what it isn't, but we haven't really figured out what the answer to the question is. The question isn't "Do you accept the responsibility principle?" That question turns out to be ambiguous because there are two different versions of the principle. And the question isn't "Do you accept the second responsibility principle?" You probably do accept the second responsibility principle. That's because you probably agree that Todd would owe Timmy some blood after he shot him and Shimp would owe McFall some bone marrow after he caused him to develop aplastic anemia. But the second responsibility principle doesn't apply to the case of Bob and Barbara. So even if we accept it, it can't help us figure out whether Bob now has the right to use Barbara's body. It's the first responsibility principle that applies to the case of Bob and Barbara. If we accept the first responsibility principle, then we really do have to agree that Bob now has the right to use Barbara's body. So the question is: Do you accept the first responsibility principle? The first responsibility principle doesn't apply to any of the cases we've considered so far. So you don't yet have a reason to answer this question one way or the other. And that's the question you need to answer to decide whether you should accept the responsibility objection.

Here's one case you can use to answer that question. Spoiler alert: it's going to be another weird one. McFall and Shimp worked together at a lab that processed a variety of toxic chemicals. One day, while Shimp was handling a particularly potent mix, he saw McFall choking. It was clear that McFall was about to die, that Shimp could save him by performing the Heimlich maneuver, and that he didn't have enough time to wash his hands before performing it. Shimp also knew if he performed the Heimlich maneuver on McFall without washing his hands first, there was a chance McFall would be exposed to the toxic chemicals he'd been handling and that McFall would later develop aplastic anemia as a result. And Shimp also happened to know from testing that had been done earlier that year that if McFall ever contracted aplastic anemia, he would need some bone marrow from Shimp in order to survive. Unfortunately, there was no one else in the lab. So Shimp's choices were to sit by and watch McFall choke to death or to perform the Heimlich maneuver on him knowing this might cause McFall to later develop aplastic anemia. Shimp went ahead and performed the maneuver and did so successfully, but McFall was exposed to the toxic chemicals in the process. As a result, he later developed aplastic anemia. You can't say I didn't warn you that it was going to be a weird story.

That was a few months ago. Now McFall will die if Shimp doesn't let him have some of his bone marrow. And Shimp has decided he doesn't want to provide it. Do you think it would be okay for the state to force Shimp to give McFall some of his bone marrow in this version of the story? I'd be really surprised if you did. If McFall had no right to use Shimp's bone marrow in the original version of the story, why would McFall suddenly have this right simply because Shimp had performed the Heimlich maneuver on him a few months ago? Why would the fact that Shimp already gave McFall the gift of some life mean he now has to give him even more? So I bet you think it would be wrong for the state to force Shimp to give McFall some of his bone marrow in this version of the story.

Let's now assume you do think this, and consider what the first responsibility principle has to say about the case. The first responsibility principle says if it's true that if you hadn't done what you did, the needy person wouldn't exist now, then you're responsible for providing them with the assistance they need. Is it true in this very weird version of the story that if Shimp hadn't done what he did then McFall wouldn't exist now? Yes, it is. If Shimp hadn't performed the Heimlich maneuver on McFall, McFall wouldn't exist now. This means if the first responsibility principle is true, then McFall now has the right to use Shimp's bone marrow. Assuming you think McFall doesn't have the right to use Shimp's bone marrow, this means you'll have to reject the first responsibility principle. And if you reject the first responsibility principle, you'll have to reject any objection to my argument that depends on it. The responsibility objection turns out to depend on the first responsibility principle. So it turns out you'll have to reject the responsibility objection.

The responsibility objection seems like a good objection at first because it seems clear at first that the responsibility principle is true and that the responsibility principle entails that Bob has a right to use Barbara's body. But once we notice the ambiguity in the principle and figure out which version of the principle we think is true and which version we think is false, it turns out the responsibility objection isn't good enough after all. The principle the objection appeals to is true in one sense, but in that sense the principle doesn't apply to the case of Bob and Barbara. In another sense, the principle does apply to the case of Bob and Barbara, but in that sense the principle isn't true. So neither version of the principle is both true and relevant to the case of Bob and Barbara. And so neither version of the principle can be used to show that Bob has the right to use Barbara's body.

# 14

## Child Support

When I've compared McFall and Shimp to a pregnant woman and her fetus, Shimp has been the pregnant woman and McFall has been the fetus. The fetus, like McFall, needs to use another person's body to go on living. The pregnant woman's body, like Shimp's, is being used to keep another person alive. But this comparison leaves someone out of the picture: the father of the fetus. What about him? The absence of a father figure in the story of McFall and Shimp makes it easy to overlook a third reason someone might have for thinking my argument doesn't work in the case of Bob and Barbara. That's because if a man freely chooses to have sex with a woman and the woman gives birth to a child as a result, the man can find himself legally obligated to support the child. And if he can find himself legally obligated to support the child even if he didn't want to become a father when he chose to have sex with the woman, then the fact that Barbara freely chose to have sex with the guy she met at the party might turn out to be enough to make it okay for the state to force her to carry her pregnancy to term after all.

Consider, for example, the case of Brent. Brent had sex with someone he met at a party, too. Her name was Betty. When Betty said she wanted to have sex with him, Brent insisted on using a condom and made clear that he had no desire to become a father. Unfortunately for Brent, the condom broke that night and Betty got pregnant. Even more unfortunately, at least as far as Brent was concerned, Betty decided to have the baby. And even more unfortunately than that, after little Billy was born, a court ordered Brent to start paying Betty child support.

If you're like most people, you'll think it's okay for the state to force Brent to pay child support in this case. And you'll think it's okay for the state to do this even though Brent didn't want to become a father when he had sex with Betty. But if that's what you think about the case of Brent, it seems you must be thinking that the fact that a person freely chooses to have sex with someone is enough to make it okay for the state to force them to support a child that results from their having sex, even if they didn't want to become a parent when they chose to have sex. And if that's what you think, then you should think the same thing about Barbara: the fact that she freely chose to have sex with the guy she met at the party is enough to make it okay for the state to force her to support Bob even if she didn't want to become a parent when she chose to have sex with the guy. And if it's okay for the state to force Barbara to support Bob, it seems like it would be okay for the state to force Barbara to carry her pregnancy to term after all.

The case of Brent and Billy can't show it would be okay for the state to prevent Alice from having an abortion. Alice didn't freely choose to have sex when she got pregnant with Al. She was raped. But the case of Brent and Billy does seem to show it would be okay for the state to prevent Barbara from having an abortion. And more generally, it seems to show it would be okay for the state to prevent a woman from having an abortion in any case where she got pregnant because she freely chose to have sex with someone. As people who are pro-life sometimes put it, the defender of abortion rights can't have it both ways here. If Barbara shouldn't be forced to support Bob, then Brent shouldn't be forced to support Billy. If Brent should be forced to support Billy, then Barbara should be forced to support Bob. I'll call this the *child support objection*.

The child support objection depends on an assumption. The assumption is that if something's enough to make it okay for the state to force you to give someone some money, then it's enough to make it okay for the state to force you to let someone use your body. The objection needs that assumption to get from the claim that Brent's role in conceiving Billy makes it okay for the state to force Brent to provide financial support to Billy to the conclusion that Barbara's role in conceiving Bob makes it okay for the state to force Barbara to provide gestational support to Bob. Without that assumption, the conclusion simply doesn't follow. And I'm pretty sure you're not going to accept that assumption once you think about what the assumption would commit you to.

If something's enough to make it okay for the state to force people to pay taxes to sponsor medical research, for example, I doubt you'll think that means it's enough to make it okay for the state to force those people to let their bodies be used in the research. If something's enough to make it okay for the state to force people to pay a fee or a fine if they behave in a certain way, I doubt you'll think that means it's enough to make it okay for the state to force people who behave in that way to give blood. If something's enough to make it okay for the state to seize someone's financial assets, I doubt you'll think that means it's enough to make it okay for the state to seize some of their bone marrow. For that matter, if you think Brent's role in conceiving Billy is enough to make it okay for the state to force Brent to provide financial support for Billy, I doubt you'll think that means it's enough to make it okay for the state to force Brent to provide bodily support for Billy—by giving him some blood or bone marrow, for example.

If you don't think these things, then you don't agree with the assumption that if something's enough to make it okay for the state to force you to give someone some money, then it's enough to make it okay for the state to force you to let someone use your body. And if you don't agree with that assumption, you can't use the case of Brent and Billy to generate a problem for my argument. The fact that it's okay for Brent to have a legal financial obligation to Billy because Brent's having sex with Betty caused Billy to exist won't mean it would be okay for Barbara to have a legal gestational obligation to Bob because Barbara's having sex with the guy she met at the party caused Bob to exist. It would mean that only if you accepted the assumption that if something's enough to make it okay for the state to force you to give someone some money, then it's enough to make it okay for the state to force you to let someone use your body. And I don't think you'll accept that assumption.

# 15

## Parents

The consent objection, the responsibility objection, and the child support objection each allow, at least for the sake of the argument, that the lesson of *McFall v. Shimp* might show it should be legal for Alice to have an abortion after she's raped. And they each try to show, in different ways, that even if this is true in the case of Alice, it's not true in the case of Barbara, Carol, Dorothy, Elaine, or any other woman who gets pregnant by freely choosing to have sex with someone. In the last three chapters, I explained each of these objections and tried to convince you not to accept them. Let's now assume for the sake of the argument that you were convinced and that there aren't any other reasons to think it should be illegal for these women to have an abortion if it should be legal for Alice to have one. If that's right, then if it should be legal for Alice to have an abortion after she's raped, it should also be legal for a woman to have an abortion if she gets pregnant by freely choosing to have sex with someone. So the question now becomes: Is there a good reason to think the lesson of *McFall v. Shimp* can't be used to show it should be legal for Alice to have an abortion after she's raped in the first place? There are a number of differences between the case of Al and Alice and the case of McFall and Shimp. So the question now becomes: Do any of these differences matter?

Here's one difference between the cases that might seem to matter: McFall was Shimp's cousin but Al is Alice's son. This might make a difference because we have special legal obligations to our own children that we don't have to other people, not even to our cousins. I could get into big trouble for neglecting to feed my children, for example, or for failing to make sure they go to school. But I don't have a legal obligation to feed your children or to make sure they go to school. And that's true even if your children are my cousins. So the fact that it would be wrong for the state to force me to provide care for someone who isn't my own son or daughter doesn't show it would be wrong for the state to force me to provide care for someone who is my own son or daughter. And so just because you think it would be wrong for the state to force Shimp to let his cousin use his body doesn't mean you have to think it would be wrong for the state to force Alice to let Al use her body. Al isn't Alice's cousin. Al is Alice's son. Since this objection appeals to the claim that parents have special legal obligations to their own children, I'll call this the *parental obligation objection*.

The basic point made by the parental obligation objection seems fair enough. A cousin isn't the same as a son or daughter, and this difference sometimes makes a difference. But does it make a difference in this case? At this point, you know the drill. Change the story of McFall and Shimp to take the difference into account and then ask whether you think the difference makes a difference. Before we can do that, though, there's a complication we have to address. That's because saying someone is your son or daughter could mean one of two things. It could mean they're your son or daughter in the biological sense. If the particular sperm or egg that led to their conception was your sperm or egg, they're your son or daughter in the biological sense. But it could mean you stand in a special kind of social relationship to them. If you adopt a child, for example, you become that child's parent in the social sense, even though you're not their parent in the biological sense. If you give a child you conceive up for adoption, the child remains your child in the biological sense but is no longer your child in the social sense. The parental obligation objection says Al has the right to use Alice's body even though McFall doesn't have the right to use Shimp's body because Al is Alice's son while McFall is merely Shimp's cousin. But because saying a person is someone's son can mean two different things, there are really two different objections here, not just one. One version of the objection appeals to a biological claim while the other appeals to a social claim. Let's consider them one at a time.

Suppose the parental obligation objection claims Al has the right to use Alice's body because Al is Alice's son in the biological sense. We can test this version of the objection by considering a version of the story where McFall is Shimp's son in the biological sense. Since Alice was raped, she didn't choose to become Al's mother in the biological sense. So we'll need a version of the story where Shimp didn't choose to become McFall's father in the biological sense, either. Here's one version that fits the bill. As always, feel free to use another if you prefer. Suppose one day while Shimp was busy at work, a stranger slipped a drug into his coffee that rendered him unconscious. While he was knocked out, the stranger removed some sperm from Shimp's body and used the sperm to fertilize an egg. The fertilized egg was then implanted in the body of a woman who carried the resulting embryo to term. She later give birth to a healthy baby boy named Robert McFall. And now, many years later, McFall has aplastic anemia and needs Shimp's bone marrow. Shimp, yet again, has declared he's unwilling to provide it. In this version of the story, McFall is Shimp's son in the biological sense, just as Al is Alice's son in the biological sense.

Now suppose McFall's lawyer goes down to the courthouse and says this to the judge: "You have to make Mr. Shimp give my client his bone marrow because he's my client's biological father." Do you think it would be okay for the judge to force Shimp to give

McFall the bone marrow in this version of the story? This strikes me as highly unlikely. If McFall had no right to use Shimp's bone marrow in the original version of the story, why would McFall suddenly have this right simply because he was conceived with sperm that had been stolen from Shimp? I can see how the fact that McFall is Shimp's son in the biological sense might have some impact on your moral reaction to the case. You might think less highly of Shimp for refusing to let McFall have the bone marrow if McFall is his own flesh and blood and not just his cousin, for example. But even if you think less highly of Shimp in this version of the story, and even if you think it would be positively immoral for him to say no in this version of the story, it's hard to believe you'll think it would be okay for the state to force Shimp to give McFall the bone marrow once he decides he's unwilling to give it. And if I'm right about that, you'll have to reject the biological version of the parental obligation objection. If you agree that the fact that McFall is Shimp's biological son doesn't give McFall the right to use Shimp's body, you'll have to agree that the fact that Al is Alice's biological son doesn't give Al the right to use Alice's body, either.

I'll move on to the social version of the parental obligation objection in a moment, but first I want to point to one other problem with the biological version. That's because some people do seem inclined to put a lot of weight on the fact that someone is another person's biological offspring. This might be particularly true among people who are pro-life. So even if most people would agree it would be wrong for the state to force Shimp to give McFall the bone marrow in this version of the story, some, and particularly some who are pro-life, might not. They might think the fact that McFall arose from Shimp's sperm is enough, all by itself, to give McFall the right to use Shimp's bone marrow. Or they might at least be willing to accept this implication if accepting it turns out to be necessary for them to consistently maintain that Al has the right to use Alice's body because Al is Alice's biological offspring.

So suppose you think of yourself as pro-life and you're considering the possibility that you might just accept this implication and endorse the claim that it would be okay for the state to force Shimp to let McFall have the bone marrow in this version of the story. If you're considering this possibility, you should first consider the case of Alison, a colleague of Alice's. One day while Alison was busy at work, a stranger slipped a drug into her coffee that rendered her unconscious. While she was knocked out, the stranger implanted an embryo in her. The embryo had been created using the sperm and egg from a couple in Chicago. The couple wanted to have a child but the wife was unable to sustain a pregnancy. They chose a male embryo and are planning to name the boy Alvin. As a result, Alison is now pregnant with Alvin and Alvin is not Alison's biological son.

If the reason you think it would be wrong for the state to let Alice have an abortion is that Al has the right to use Alice's body because Al is Alice's biological son, then you'll have to agree the state should let Alison have an abortion because Alvin isn't Alison's biological son and so doesn't have the right to use Alison's body. And, more generally, you'll have to agree it should be legal for a woman to have an abortion as long as the fetus she's carrying was created from someone else's egg. Do you think this? I'd be surprised if you do. I don't think I've ever heard of a pro-life person who thought abortion should be legal as long as the fetus wasn't biologically related to the pregnant woman. And if you don't think this, then you can't accept the biological version of the parental obligation objection.

Now let's turn to the second version of the parental obligation objection. The second version claims Al has the right to use Alice's body because Al is Alice's son in the social sense. We can test this objection by considering a version of the story of McFall and Shimp where McFall is Shimp's son in the social sense. So suppose over thirty years ago, Shimp and his wife adopted little baby Robert McFall. Shimp was an engaged and loving father and they had a great relationship while McFall was growing up. McFall has now contracted aplastic anemia, and although Shimp isn't biologically related to McFall, it turns out he's the only one who can provide the bone marrow McFall now needs. Would it be okay for the state to force Shimp to give McFall the bone marrow in this version of the story?

My guess is you'll say no. You may be particularly appalled at the thought of Shimp turning his back on McFall in this version of the story, but my guess is you'll be even more appalled at the thought of the state's forcing Shimp to let McFall have the bone marrow if Shimp refuses to give it to him. Let's assume I'm right about that. In that case, your response to the social version of the parental obligation objection should be simple. If the fact that McFall is Shimp's son in the social sense doesn't give him the right to use Shimp's body, then the claim that Al is Alice's son in the social sense won't be enough to show that Al has the right to use Alice's body, either.

But suppose my guess is wrong. Suppose you think it really would be okay for the state to force Shimp to give McFall the bone marrow in this version of the story. If that's what you think, what should you think about the social version of the parental obligation objection? What you should think depends on why you think McFall has the right to Shimp's bone marrow in this version of the story. As far as I can tell, there are only two features of the story you could point to. First, you might point to the fact that by adopting McFall, Shimp agreed to provide care for McFall. That makes this version of the story different from every other version I've told. You might think if Shimp doesn't give McFall the bone marrow now, he's violating an agreement he made earlier and that it's okay for the state to step in and enforce the terms of this agreement. Second, you might point to the fact that McFall and Shimp have had a loving relationship for many years and think this has an impact on what Shimp now owes McFall.

I have doubts about whether either of these features of the story could be enough to make it okay for the state to force Shimp to give McFall the bone marrow. But I can't see any other reason to think it would be okay for the state to do this. So if you do think it would be okay for the state to force Shimp to give McFall the bone marrow in this version of the story, it seems that it would have to be because you think two things. First, you think being Shimp's son in the social sense means being someone Shimp has agreed to take care of, being someone Shimp has had a loving parental relationship with, or both. Second, you think being Shimp's son in this social sense is enough to give McFall the right to use Shimp's body.

But if this is what you think about this version of the story of McFall and Shimp, you should go back to the case of Al and Alice and ask whether Al is Alice's son in the social sense. It's clear Al is Alice's son in the biological sense because Al was conceived from one of Alice's eggs. And it's clear Al would be Alice's son in the social sense if she chose to carry her pregnancy to term and take Al home rather than to put him up for adoption. Taking a child you've created into your home rather than putting the child up for adoption amounts to agreeing to be that child's parent in the social sense just as adopting a child you didn't create does. What isn't clear is whether Al is Alice's son in the social sense right now, while she's pregnant with him. Whether Al is Alice's son in the social sense while Alice is pregnant with Al depends on what we think it takes to be someone's son in the social sense. As far as I can tell, if you think McFall would have the right to Shimp's bone marrow because McFall is Shimp's son in the social sense, you must think that what it takes to be a person's son in the social sense is for them to be either someone the person has agreed to take care of, someone the person has had a loving parental relationship with, or both.

But if that's what you think, you'll have to conclude that while Alice is pregnant with Al, Al isn't Alice's son in the social sense. Even Barbara, who freely chose to have sex with the guy she met at the party, never agreed that she'd care for the fetus she conceived if she got pregnant as a result of her choice. Alice, who was raped while she was unconscious, certainly didn't agree to this, either explicitly or implicitly. And Alice hasn't engaged in a loving parental relationship with Al, either. So whether you think what's required to make McFall Shimp's son in the social sense has to do with consent, a shared history of loving interactions, or both, you'll have to conclude that Al isn't Alice's son in the social sense. And if Al isn't Alice's son in the social sense, you'll have to reject the social version of the parental obligation objection regardless of whether you think being someone's son in the social sense is enough to give you the right to use their body.

In short, Al is Alice's son in the biological sense, but being Alice's son in the biological sense doesn't give Al the right to use Alice's body. Being someone's son in the social sense probably doesn't give you the right to use their body either, but even if it does, the very reasons for thinking so are reasons for concluding that Al isn't Alice's son in the social sense. So neither the biological sense nor the social sense is one on which it's true both that Al is Alice's son and that being Alice's son in that sense gives Al the right to use Alice's body. And so neither version of the parental obligation objection is successful.

## 16

## Children

Okay, I might have cheated a little bit in that last chapter. I admitted we have stronger legal obligations to our own children than we have to other people, and I admitted this seemed to pose a problem for my argument. Just because the state shouldn't force Shimp to keep his cousin alive doesn't mean it shouldn't force a pregnant woman to keep her son or daughter alive. I then drew a distinction between two versions of this parental obligation objection. In each case, I asked you to consider a story where McFall was Shimp's son in the relevant sense. And in each case, I tried to use the story to convince you that the version of the parental obligation objection was unsuccessful.

But Robert McFall was an adult. When I asked you to imagine a version of the story where Shimp refuses to let his son have some of his bone marrow, I was asking you to picture a story where Shimp was refusing to help his adult son. And that isn't really a fair way to test the parental obligation objection. After all, when I admitted we have stronger legal obligations to our own children than we have to other people, I wasn't talking about our adult children. You can get into big trouble with the law if you neglect to make sure your 5-year-old is eating enough. If you don't make sure your 35-year-old is eating enough, they're pretty much on their own as far as the law is concerned. The real point of the parental obligation objection wasn't merely to say the fetus is the unborn son or daughter of the pregnant woman but to say the fetus is her unborn *child*. In whatever sense it's true that Al is Alice's son, he's Alice's baby son, not Alice's adult son. And since parents have stronger legal obligations to their children when their children are very young than they have to their children when their children are adults, this difference that I glossed over in the previous chapter might turn out to make a difference. A critic of my argument would be entitled to insist that if we're going to really assume the fetus is a person, we have to assume the fetus is a child.

So it looks like we need yet another version of the story of McFall and Shimp. This time, we need a version where McFall isn't just Shimp's son but is Shimp's baby son. And since there turned out to be two versions of the parental obligation objection, we'll need two versions of this new story, one where McFall is Shimp's baby son in the biological sense and one where McFall is Shimp's baby son in the social sense. If you agreed with what I said in the previous chapter, I'm pretty sure these changes to the story won't convince you to change your mind about either version of the parental obligation objection. But let's check and see.

I'll start with a version of the story where McFall is Shimp's baby son in the biological sense. So suppose again that a stranger slipped a drug into Shimp's coffee, removed some sperm from Shimp's body while he was unconscious, and used the sperm to fertilize an egg that was later implanted in a woman's body. But this time, instead of saying it's now many years later, let's say it's just a few months after the woman gave birth to a little baby boy named Robert McFall. The baby developed aplastic anemia shortly after he was born and he now needs Shimp's bone marrow. Do you think it would be okay for Judge Flaherty to force Shimp to give McFall the bone marrow in this version of the story? I doubt it. You might think it takes someone with an especially hard heart to say no to giving bone marrow to a little baby who needs it. But if that's the kind of heart Shimp has, it's hard to believe you'll think it would be okay for the state to force Shimp to give it to him. If McFall didn't have the right to Shimp's bone marrow in the first version of the story, where McFall was conceived with sperm that had been stolen from Shimp, it's hard to see why he would have it in this second version just because McFall is much younger in this version. It's true babies have some legal rights that adults don't have, but it's hard to believe the right to use the bone marrow of their biological parents should be one of them. If that's your reaction to this case, then the difference between babies and adults won't be enough to save the biological version of the parental obligation objection.

Now let's consider a version of the story where McFall is Shimp's baby son in the social sense. Here we can take the version of the story where Shimp and his wife adopted little baby Robert McFall and instead of saying this happened over thirty years ago, we can say it happened just a few months ago. The baby has now contracted aplastic anemia and although Shimp isn't biologically related to him, it turns out he's the only one who can provide the bone marrow the baby now needs. Shimp, yet again, declares he's unwilling to provide the bone marrow and McFall's lawyer, yet again, goes to court to get Judge Flaherty to order Shimp to provide it. Would it be okay for the state to force Shimp to give McFall the bone marrow in the version of the story where Shimp adopted McFall as a baby?

As turned out to be the case with the first version of the adoption story, it doesn't really matter what your answer is here. If you think it would be wrong for the state to force Shimp to give McFall the bone marrow in this version of the story, then you'll agree that even if Al is Alice's baby son in the social sense, this won't be enough to make it okay for the state to force Alice to let Al use her body. But even if you think it would be okay for the state to force Shimp to give McFall the bone marrow in this version of the story, this still won't help to rescue the social version of the parental obligation objection. That's because if you do think this, it will almost certainly be because you think it matters that Shimp agreed to care for the little baby when he adopted him or that he had a loving parental relationship with the baby for at least a few months before the baby came to need to use his body. And since neither of these things is true about Al and Alice, your reason for thinking baby McFall is Shimp's son in the social sense will show that baby Al isn't Alice's son in the social sense. And if baby Al isn't Alice's son in the social sense, then the social version of the parental obligation objection will again be unsuccessful. So even after we take into account the difference between babies and adults, we'll still see that both versions of the parental obligation objection are unsuccessful. I've said if you agree that Judge Flaherty made the right call in the case of *McFall v. Shimp*, you should agree that it would be wrong for the state to prevent Alice from having an abortion. Neither version of the parental obligation objection provides a good reason to think I was wrong about that, even after we take into account the difference between adults and babies.

## 17

# Natural Purposes

Here's another difference between the case of McFall and Shimp and the case of Al and Alice. It seems unnatural for Shimp to use his bone marrow to keep McFall alive. But it seems natural for Alice to use her uterus to keep Al alive. We might say the purpose of a woman's uterus is to gestate the fetuses she conceives, while the purpose of a person's bone marrow isn't to keep other people alive. Or we might put it this way: a woman's uterus is for gestating the fetuses she conceives, while a person's bone marrow isn't for keeping other people alive. If that's right, then a critic of my argument might object as follows: Al has the right to use Alice's uterus because that's what Alice's uterus is there for, but McFall doesn't have the right to use Shimp's bone marrow because that's not what Shimp's bone marrow is there for. It would be wrong for the state to force Shimp to let McFall use his bone marrow because McFall doesn't have the right to use Shimp's bone marrow. But that doesn't mean it would be wrong for the state to force Alice to let Al use her uterus because Al has the right to use Alice's uterus. Al has the right to use Alice's uterus because that's what Alice's uterus is for. Since this objection claims Al has the right to use Alice's uterus because it's natural for Al to use it, I'll call it the *natural right objection*.

What should you think about this objection? That depends on what you think about the claim that a woman's uterus is for gestating the fetuses she conceives. You might think this claim is a bunch of hooey. That's because you might think it makes sense to say a human organ is for some particular purpose only if someone designed it for that purpose, and you might think no one designed the human uterus. If that's what you think, you should think the natural right objection is a bunch of hooey, too, since the natural right objection depends on this claim. But you might think it makes perfect sense to say a woman's uterus is for gestating the fetuses she conceives. You might think God created people as they are and that he designed the human uterus for women to use to gestate the fetuses they conceive. Or you might think people are the product of natural selection and that it makes perfect sense to say a human organ is for a particular purpose if it evolved via natural selection because it served that purpose. If you think a woman's uterus is for gestating the fetuses she conceives for one of these reasons, what should you conclude about the natural right objection?

Suppose you think God created people as they are and that he designed the human uterus for women to use to gestate the fetuses they conceive. And suppose, just to be clear, when you say God designed the uterus for this purpose, you mean at least in part that God intended women to use their uteruses for this purpose. In that case, you should think Alice would violate God's will if she had an abortion. Should you also think it would be okay for the state to make it illegal for Alice to have an abortion? That depends on whether you think it would be okay for the state to make it illegal to do any other act you think violates God's will. Depending on what religious tradition you belong to, you may think that some or all of the following acts also violate God's will: masturbation, contraception, premarital sex, anal sex, oral sex, adultery, idolatry, blasphemy, working on the Sabbath, and taking God's name in vain. If you think it would be okay for the state to ban any of these acts if they violate God's will, and you think the same goes for any other act you think violates God's will, then you should think it would be okay for the state to prevent Alice from having an abortion. I'm guessing relatively few religious people reading this book will think it would be okay for the state to ban every act they think violates God's will. And if you don't think this would be okay, you can't endorse the natural right objection by appealing to the claim that God designed the human uterus for women to use to gestate the fetuses they conceive.

If you do think it would be okay for the state to ban every act you think violates God's will, I'll say something in a moment about why you still shouldn't accept the natural right objection. But since what I'll have to say about that will also apply to those who favor the second reason for thinking a woman's uterus is for gestating the fetuses she conceives, let me say something about that second reason first. So suppose you think people are the product of natural selection and that it makes perfect sense to say a human organ is for a particular purpose if it evolved via natural selection in the way it did because it served that purpose. And you think it's clear the human uterus evolved in the way it did because evolving in that way served the purpose of enabling women to gestate the fetuses they conceived. In that case, you should think that if Alice had an abortion, she would fail to use her uterus for the purpose it evolved to serve. Should you also think it would be okay for the state to make it illegal for Alice to have an abortion?

That depends on whether you think it would be okay for the state to make it illegal to do any other act that involves failing to use a human organ for the purpose it evolved to serve. Assuming the penis didn't evolve in order to enable men to masturbate, for example, you'd have to agree that it would be okay for the state to make it illegal for men to use their penises to masturbate. I doubt you think that would be okay. You might think you could avoid accepting this implication by saying you should be allowed to sometimes fail to use your organs for their intended purpose as long as you sometimes use them for their intended purpose. But then you'd have to say it would be okay for the state to prevent Alice from having an abortion if she never used her uterus to gestate the fetuses she conceived but wrong for the state to prevent her from having an abortion if she'd already used her uterus to carry at least one pregnancy to term. And you'd have to say it would be okay for the state to make it illegal for men to masturbate if they never used their penis to conceive a child but wrong for the state to make it illegal for men to masturbate if they had already used their penis to conceive a child. I doubt anyone believes these things. So while many people will agree that natural selection can make it meaningful to say a human organ is there to serve a particular purpose, I don't think many of them will think this is a good way to reject the natural right objection, either.

I've tried to convince you so far that the claim that a woman's uterus is for gestating the fetuses she conceives isn't a good basis for defending the natural right objection regardless of whether you accept the claim for religious or evolutionary reasons. But let's suppose you're not convinced. Let's suppose you find yourself inclined to think two things: that a woman's uterus is for gestating the fetuses she conceives and that this fact matters when comparing the case of McFall and Shimp with the case of Al and Alice. You're inclined to think McFall has no right to use Shimp's bone marrow because that's not what Shimp's bone marrow is for and to think Al does have the right to use Alice's uterus because that's what Alice's uterus is for. If you find yourself inclined to think these things even after what I've said so far, I want to point out a problem with this kind of thinking that's likely to lead you to reject it.

So let's return to the case of Alison. In case you've forgotten her, Alison is the colleague of Alice's who was also rendered unconscious when a stranger slipped a drug into her coffee. While Alison was knocked out, the stranger implanted an embryo in her that had been created using the sperm and egg from a couple in Chicago. They chose a male embryo and are planning to name the boy Alvin. As a result, Alison is now pregnant with Alvin but Alison didn't conceive Alvin. If the reason you think Al has the right to use Alice's uterus while McFall doesn't have the right to use Shimp's bone marrow is that Alice's uterus is for gestating the fetuses she conceives while Shimp's bone marrow isn't for keeping other people alive, then you'll have to agree that Alvin doesn't have the right to use Alison's uterus. That's because Alison didn't conceive Alvin and so her uterus isn't for gestating him. It will be consistent for you to say both that the state should force Alice to let Al use her uterus and that it would be wrong for the state to force Shimp to let McFall use his bone marrow, but then you'll have to say it would be wrong for the state to force Alison to let Alvin use her uterus. And, more generally, you'll have to agree that it should be legal for a woman to have an abortion as long as she didn't conceive the fetus she's carrying.

Do you think this? It seems unlikely. Regardless of whether you consider yourself pro-life, pro-choice, or somewhere in between, it's hard to believe you'll think this difference between Alice and Alison could make a difference. You might think the state should allow both to have an abortion or you might think it shouldn't allow either to have an abortion, but it's hard to believe you'll think it should allow Alison to have an abortion while preventing Alice from having one. And if you don't think that, you can't endorse the natural right objection. You might be tempted to think this isn't a big problem since hardly any abortions involve cases like Alison's. But the numbers don't matter. The problem with the natural right objection is a matter of principle, not of practice. Even if Alison's case is extremely rare, it's still true that if you don't think the fact that Alice's uterus is for gestating Al while Alison's uterus isn't for gestating Alvin makes a difference, then you can't think the fact that Alice's uterus is for gestating Al while Shimp's bone marrow isn't for keeping McFall alive makes a difference. A contradiction in your thinking is a contradiction in your thinking regardless of how many actual cases there are that prove it. And if you don't think the fact that Alice's uterus is for gestating Al while Shimp's bone marrow isn't for keeping McFall alive makes a difference, then you can't use the difference to explain why it would be wrong for the state to force Shimp to let McFall use his bone marrow but not wrong for the state to force Alice to let Al use her uterus. As a result, you'll have to reject the natural right objection.

Now you might think there's a way around this problem. You might think that instead of saying a woman's uterus is for gestating the fetuses she conceives, we should say a woman's uterus is for gestating any fetus that needs to use her uterus, or maybe just for gestating any fetus that's already using her uterus. If Alison's uterus is for gestating any fetus that needs to use her uterus, or for gestating any fetus that's already using her uterus, then it will turn out that Alison's uterus is for gestating Alvin after all and that Alvin really does have a right to use Alison's uterus as a result. And that would mean you could agree with the natural right objection without having to think Alison should be allowed to have an abortion while Alice shouldn't.

But this way around the problem with the natural right objection won't work. If we say Alison's uterus is for gestating any fetus that needs to use her uterus, or for gestating any fetus that's already using her uterus, then we'll have to say the same thing about Shimp's bone marrow. The primary function of bone marrow is to produce blood cells. If we say Alison's uterus is just for gestating Alison's fetuses, we can say Shimp's bone marrow is just for producing blood cells for Shimp. But if we say Alison's uterus is for gestating any fetus that needs to use her uterus, or for gestating any fetus that's already using her uterus, then we'll have to say Shimp's bone marrow is for generating blood cells for anyone who needs to use his bone marrow, or for generating blood cells for anyone who's already using his bone marrow. And if Shimp's bone marrow is for generating blood cells for anyone who needs to use his bone marrow, or for generating blood cells for anyone who's already using his bone marrow, then McFall will have just as much right to use Shimp's bone marrow as Alvin will have to use Alison's uterus. I can't see any reason for saying Alison's uterus is for gestating other people's fetuses in these ways while at the same time insisting that Shimp's bone marrow is only for generating blood cells for Shimp. If God intended women to let other people's fetuses use their uteruses why wouldn't God intend them to let other people use their bone marrow? If natural selection says the uterus is for gestating other people's fetuses, why wouldn't it say bone marrow is for producing blood cells for other people? I can't see a good answer to either of these questions. If you can't either, you can't accept this way of trying to get around the problem that Alice and Alison pose for the natural right objection. And if you can't find any other way to get around the problem, then you can't accept the natural right objection.

# 18

## Cause of Death

Strictly speaking, if Shimp is disconnected from the bone marrow transferring machine, the process of disconnecting him won't kill McFall. What will kill McFall is his aplastic anemia. Disconnecting Shimp from the machine will simply allow the disease to run its course. But if Alice has an abortion, it's the abortion itself that will kill Al. Al will be cut into pieces before he's removed from Alice's uterus, for example, or cut into pieces in the process of being removed. So if Shimp is disconnected from the bone marrow transferring machine, he'll let McFall die, but if Alice has an abortion, her having an abortion will kill Al. This seems to be another difference between the two cases.

And it doesn't just seem to be another difference. It seems like the kind of difference that might matter. Generally speaking, if you kill someone, you've done something illegal, but if you simply let someone die, you haven't. If you give people poisoned food, for example, you're probably going to get into big trouble with the law. If you decide not to donate food to people who will die without it, you're probably not. Same goes for pushing a fellow cruise passenger overboard compared to not fishing them out of the water if they accidentally fall in. Or stabbing someone until they bleed to death compared to refusing to give blood to someone who will bleed to death without it. And most people seem to agree that this general feature of the law is as it should be: you really should have a strong legal duty not to kill other people, but as a general matter you shouldn't really have a legal duty to go around saving other people.

This difference between killing and letting die seems to pose a problem for my argument because a critic might be justified in saying something like this: it would be wrong for the state to force Shimp to stay connected to the bone marrow transferring machine because Shimp should have the right to let McFall die and disconnecting himself from the machine would simply involve letting McFall die. But that doesn't mean it would be wrong for the state to force Alice to carry her pregnancy to term because Alice doesn't have the right to kill Al and if she has an abortion Al will be killed.

If this objection is right, then the difference between the cause of death in the case of McFall and Shimp and the cause of death in the case of Al and Alice turns out to make a difference. It isn't just the fact that Al has a right to life that gives him the right to keep using Alice's uterus. It's the fact that Al has a right to life plus the fact that Alice would have to kill Al to make him stop using her uterus that gives Al the right to keep using Alice's uterus. Since Shimp can make McFall stop using his bone marrow by letting McFall die rather than by killing him, this means McFall doesn't have the right to keep using Shimp's bone marrow even though Al does have the right to keep using Alice's uterus. And if that's right, my argument falls apart at this point. Agreeing that it would be wrong for the state to force Shimp to let McFall use his bone marrow will no longer commit you to agreeing that it would be wrong for the state to force Alice to let Al use her uterus.

We can test this objection in two ways. One, yet again, is to change the story of McFall and Shimp. Another is to change the story of Al and Alice. Let's start with Al and Alice. Up to this point, I haven't said anything about what kind of abortion Alice is planning to have because that didn't seem to matter. But now let's get more specific. Most methods of abortion involve killing the fetus either before or during the process of removing it from the pregnant woman's uterus. Dilation and curettage is a common example. First, the woman's cervix is dilated to enable a surgical instrument to be inserted and then the instrument is used to scrape out the contents of her uterus. Let's assume if Alice has a dilation and curettage abortion, Al will be cut into pieces by this instrument and will be dead before the abortion is completed. On that assumption, the critic seems entitled to say that disconnecting Shimp from the bone marrow transferring machine merely lets McFall die, that Alice's having an abortion kills Al, and that if the difference between killing and letting die makes a difference, then saying it would be wrong to prevent Shimp from being disconnected doesn't commit you to saying it would be wrong to prevent Alice from having an abortion. I'll call this the *killing versus letting die objection*.

If the objection to my argument is understood this way, we can change the story of Al and Alice by changing the method of abortion Alice would use. A hysterotomy abortion, for example, involves removing the fetus while it's still alive through an abdominal incision in the uterus. It's like having a caesarean section, but with a smaller incision. Assuming the fetus isn't viable when the abortion is performed, it will die soon after it's removed because it will no longer be receiving the life support it needs from the pregnant woman's body. And then there's the abortion pill. This method involves two drugs. One is mifepristone. It blocks the production of the hormone progesterone and causes the lining of the uterus to deteriorate as a result. The other is misoprostol. It induces contractions and causes the woman to have a miscarriage. The combination of the two prevents the uterus from providing the fetus with the support it needs and results in the fetus being expelled from the uterus where it will no longer be able to survive. So neither the abortion pill nor abortion by hysterotomy kills the fetus. They cause the fetus to exit the woman's uterus and to die as a result. Let's change the story of Al and Alice, then, and say if Alice has an abortion, she'll have a hysterotomy abortion. Al will be removed from her uterus while he's still alive and will die shortly after.

Now before I ask whether you think changing the method of abortion from one that kills Al to one that lets Al die makes a difference in terms of whether the state should allow it, I should note that you might think this is a misleading way of putting things. You might think removing a fetus intact from a woman's uterus when there's no way the fetus can survive without using her uterus really amounts to killing the fetus and not just to letting the fetus die. You might think, for example, that removing a fetus from a woman's uterus in this way is like unplugging a kidney patient from the dialysis machine he needs. If an intruder breaks into a hospital and unplugs a kidney patient from his dialysis machine, we could say the intruder simply lets the patient die of his kidney ailment, but it would probably seem more natural to say the intruder kills him. In the same way, and for the same reason, if Alice has a hysterotomy abortion, you might think it's more accurate to say the abortion kills Al than to say it simply lets Al die.

If you're inclined to think a hysterotomy abortion would kill Al for this reason, I won't argue with you. But if that's what you think, you'll have to say disconnecting Shimp from the bone marrow transferring machine would kill McFall and would not simply let McFall die. After all, disconnecting Shimp from the machine would remove the life support McFall needs just as surely as Alice's hysterotomy abortion would remove the life support Al needs. And if disconnecting Shimp kills McFall, then the fact that Alice's abortion kills Al won't matter. If it would be wrong for the state to prevent Shimp from being disconnected from the machine even though disconnecting Shimp would kill

McFall, then the fact that having an abortion would kill Al can't be enough to make it okay for the state to prevent Alice from having an abortion. If the killing versus letting die objection is to have any chance of succeeding, then, the person who defends the objection will have to agree that if Alice has a hysterotomy abortion, that will involve letting Al die rather than killing Al. Assuming that's so, let me now ask whether you think this change to the story of Al and Alice makes a difference. In terms of whether it would be okay for the state to prevent Alice from having an abortion, that is, do you think it matters whether she would have a dilation and curettage abortion or a hysterotomy abortion?

My guess is you won't think it makes a difference. If you're pro-choice and you think it would be wrong for the state to prevent Alice from having a dilation and curettage abortion, you'll probably think it would be wrong for the state to prevent her from having a hysterotomy abortion, too. If you think Alice should be allowed to have an abortion that involves killing Al, why wouldn't you think she should be allowed to have an abortion that merely allows Al to die? And if you're pro-life and you think the state should prevent Alice from having a dilation and curettage abortion, you'll probably think the state should prevent her from having a hysterotomy abortion, too. It's pretty rare, after all, to come across a pro-life person who thinks abortion should be legal as long as the fetus dies a few minutes after being removed from the woman's uterus rather than a few minutes before. If you're pro-life, you might think dilation and curettage abortion is morally worse than hysterotomy abortion, or morally worse than the abortion pill, and you might think this because you think killing a fetus is morally worse than letting a fetus die, but it's unlikely you'll think this difference makes a difference in terms of whether the abortion should be legal. If you think dilation and curettage abortion should be illegal, you'll probably think hysterotomy abortion and the abortion pill should be illegal, too.

Now suppose I'm right about this. If I am right, then you can't accept the killing versus letting die objection. If you don't think the fact that dilation and curettage would kill Al while hysterotomy would let Al die makes a difference in terms of whether they should be legal, then you can't think the fact that dilation and curettage would kill Al while disconnecting Shimp would let McFall die can make a difference in terms of whether they should be legal. And if you don't think the fact that dilation and curettage would kill Al while disconnecting Shimp would let McFall die makes a difference in terms of whether they should be legal, then you are rejecting the killing versus letting die objection.

But suppose I'm wrong about this and you think the difference between dilation and curettage abortion and hysterotomy abortion really does make a difference in terms of whether the abortion should be legal. In that case, you should say letting Shimp be disconnected from the bone marrow transferring machine is like letting Alice have a hysterotomy abortion but not like letting Alice have a dilation and curettage abortion. And if that's what you think, you should think it would be okay for the state to prevent Alice from having a dilation and curettage abortion but wrong for the state to prevent Alice from having a hysterotomy abortion. And more generally, you should think it would be okay for the state to prevent Alice from having an abortion that would kill Al prior to or in the process of removing him but wrong for the state to prevent Alice from having an abortion that would result in Al being removed or expelled from her body and then dying from a lack of life support.

This would be an unusual position to end up with, and one that won't fully satisfy people on either side of the abortion debate. On the one hand, this position says it would be okay for the state to prohibit a number of methods of abortion that are currently legal. That won't make pro-choice people happy. On the other hand, it says every woman should have the legal right to have an abortion, as long as she uses some methods of abortion and not others. That won't make pro-life people happy. Still, unusual as it might be, that's the position you should take if you think the difference between killing and letting die makes a difference in terms of whether an abortion should be legal and you agree that some abortion methods involve killing the fetus while others involve removing it and letting it die. And remember, if you try to argue that even hysterotomy or the abortion pill involves killing Al because it removes Al from what he needs to go on living, then you'll have to say that disconnecting Shimp kills McFall because it removes McFall from what he needs to go on living. And if disconnecting Shimp kills McFall, then the killing versus letting die objection to my argument can't get off the ground in the first place.

I'm not sure how many people will end up holding this position. But in case you're one of them, let me emphasize that even if you end up holding it, you're still agreeing with the basic claim I'm trying to defend in this book. The main goal of this book is to convince you that abortion should be legal. That doesn't have to mean every method of abortion should be legal. Lots of things are legal if they're done in some ways and not in other ways. Medically speaking, the premature termination of a pregnancy is an abortion regardless of whether it leads the fetus to die before, during, or shortly after the procedure. So if you think it should be legal for Alice to have her pregnancy terminated prior to viability as long as it's done in some ways and not others, then you still think it should be legal for Alice to have an abortion prior to viability and so still agree with the basic claim I'm trying to defend in this book.

Okay, so much for testing the killing versus letting die objection by changing the story of Al and Alice. What if we change the story of McFall and Shimp instead? In the versions of the story I've told so far, if Shimp declines to let McFall use his bone marrow, he merely lets McFall die. But what if we change the story so that in order for Shimp to stop letting McFall use his bone marrow, McFall has to be killed? Would that make a difference? If so, then we seem to have a problem all over again.

It's tempting to think we can answer this question by changing the story to one where the doctor would have to cut McFall into pieces either before or during the process of disconnecting Shimp from the bone marrow transferring machine. But there's a problem with using this version of the story. The problem is if we picture McFall being cut into pieces while Shimp is being disconnected from the machine, we'll probably assume, at least at some level, that McFall is being made to suffer. If we end up thinking it would be okay for the state to prevent the doctor from disconnecting Shimp from the machine in this case, it might be because we think it would be appropriate for the state to prevent McFall from suffering. And since most abortions take place well before the fetus can feel pain, this would render our judgment irrelevant to the question we're trying to answer. If we want to test the claim that the difference between killing and letting die poses a problem for my argument, then, we'll need a case where it will be clear to us that disconnecting Shimp from the machine involves killing McFall and also clear to us that disconnecting Shimp from the machine won't cause McFall any pain.

So let's say this instead. McFall's in a coma right now. He can't feel a thing. If Shimp doesn't give him the bone marrow he needs, McFall will die before he wakes up. The machine is designed to prevent Shimp from being disconnected from it as long as McFall is connected to it. So the only way the doctor can disconnect Shimp from the machine is to disconnect McFall from it first.

The only way the doctor can disconnect McFall from the machine is to make a small incision in McFall's back that will inevitably cause an infection. Because of his weakened condition, McFall will be unable to fend off the infection and will die as a result. So if the doctor disconnects Shimp from the machine, McFall will die from the infection caused by the doctor's act, not from the aplastic anemia. The doctor's act of disconnecting Shimp will therefore kill McFall, and kill him painlessly. This change to the story makes the case of disconnecting Shimp just like the case of Alice's having a dilation and curettage abortion in terms of the difference between painlessly killing someone and painlessly letting someone die. Disconnecting Shimp would painlessly kill McFall. Aborting Al by dilation and curettage would painlessly kill Al. So it seems like the right kind of case to consider here. The question, then, is whether it would be okay for the state to force Shimp to let McFall continue using his bone marrow in this version of the story where disconnecting McFall would involve causing McFall's death and not simply letting his death occur.

You again have two ways to go here. One is to say Shimp should still be allowed to be disconnected from the machine even if it means causing McFall to die from a lethal infection rather than allowing him to die from the aplastic anemia. If that's your view, then my argument will still be in good shape as far as you're concerned. If you think it would be wrong to prevent Shimp from being disconnected by a method that involves painlessly causing McFall's death rather than painlessly allowing it, then you can't say the fact that Alice's having a dilation and curettage abortion would painlessly cause Al's death rather than painlessly allow it makes it okay to prevent Alice from having that kind of abortion. And it seems likely enough that this will be your response. Since McFall has no right to the life support he's receiving and would be dead if he weren't receiving it, you may well think Shimp is entitled to withdraw that support even if doing so involves taking McFall's life. Since McFall has no right to remain alive at Shimp's expense, after all, doing so would not make McFall any worse off than he has the right to be.

But let's suppose that's not your response. Let's suppose while you agree it would be wrong for the state to prevent Shimp from being disconnected in a way that involves allowing McFall to die of his aplastic anemia, you think it would be okay for the state to prevent him from being disconnected in a way that would involve causing McFall to develop and die from a fatal infection. Indeed, let's suppose you think it would be positively wrong for the state *not* to prevent Shimp from doing this. If that's what you think, then you should think the state shouldn't prevent Alice from having a hysterotomy abortion or prevent her from taking the abortion pill, since that would be like preventing Shimp from letting McFall die, but that the state should prevent Alice from having a dilation and curettage abortion, since that would be like preventing Shimp from causing McFall's death. As I mentioned before, this is a somewhat unusual position to take, and I'm not sure how many people will end up taking it, but the important thing to note again is that even if you end up taking it, this still won't pose a problem for the basic claim I'm making in this book. The goal of this book is to convince you that abortion should be legal. That doesn't have to mean every method of abortion should be legal. So if you think it should be legal for Alice to have an abortion as long as it's done in some ways but not if it's done in other ways, you still think it should be legal for Alice to have an abortion and so still agree with the basic claim I'm making in this book.

Rather than trying to argue you out of this position if that's the position you find yourself in, then, let me just note one complication you'll have to address. I'm certainly no expert, but from what I can tell, the abortion pill is about as safe and effective as it gets. So if the state tells Alice she can have an abortion but only if she uses the abortion pill instead of having a dilation and curettage abortion, it probably won't be that big a deal for Alice. She may well prefer to take the pill anyway. But generally speaking, the abortion pill is recommended only in cases where it's been ten weeks or less since the woman's last period. Suppose Alice has been pregnant for considerably longer than that and she isn't able to use the pill. And suppose the state tells her she can still have an abortion by hysterotomy, since that would result in Al's being removed alive and left to die, but she can't have a dilation and curettage abortion because that would involve Al's being killed before or during the process of being removed. That might be a big deal for Alice because having a hysterotomy abortion is considerably riskier for her than having a dilation and curettage abortion. That's why abortion by hysterotomy is extremely rare. And you might well think this makes a difference. You might think it would be okay for the state to say Alice can only have an abortion that lets Al die rather than one that kills Al if either choice would be equally safe for Alice. That's because you might think there's an important enough difference between killing and letting die in cases where all else is equal. But even if you do think that, you still might want to say something different if limiting Alice's options in this way will make things significantly more dangerous for Alice without making things any better for Al. Do you still think the state should ban dilation and curettage but allow hysterotomy if all else is importantly unequal in this respect?

If you're inclined to think that as a general matter, the state should only let Alice have an abortion if it involves letting Al die rather than killing him, and if you're wondering whether you should make an exception to this restriction in the case where limiting Alice's choice to a hysterotomy would make things significantly more dangerous for Alice, you should turn once more to the case of McFall and Shimp. So suppose Shimp tells the doctor he wants to be disconnected from the bone marrow transferring machine and the doctor says there are two ways that can be done. The first method will kill McFall by making a small incision in his back that will result in a lethal infection, and the second method will enable McFall to briefly survive the process of disconnection before he succumbs to the aplastic anemia. McFall is in a coma, so it won't make any difference to him which method the doctor uses. But suppose it turns out the second method would be significantly more dangerous to Shimp than the first. Do you think it would be okay for the state to say Shimp can only be disconnected from the machine at this point if the doctor uses the second and more dangerous method since that would result in letting McFall die from the aplastic anemia rather than causing him to develop an infection that would kill him instead?

I have to admit I have trouble seeing why Shimp should be forced to undergo the more dangerous disconnection procedure given that McFall has no right to use Shimp's bone marrow in the first place and that McFall will die either way. If you found yourself in Shimp's situation, I suspect you'd feel entitled to choose the safer option to disconnect yourself and that if you found yourself in McFall's situation, you wouldn't care which option Shimp chose. So if I had to guess, I'd say you'll think it would be wrong for the state to limit Shimp to the more dangerous disconnection procedure. Even if you think the difference between killing and letting die makes a moral difference, and even if you think it should make a legal difference when all else is equal, you'll think it doesn't make a big enough difference to justify the state's imposing a significantly increased risk of harm on Shimp when all else isn't equal. If it should be legal to disconnect Shimp by the more dangerous method, that is, you'll agree it should be legal to disconnect him by the less dangerous method, since that would be safer for him and no worse for McFall. And if that's what you think about this version of the story of McFall and Shimp, that's what you should think about the case of Al and Alice. Even if you think the difference between killing and letting die makes a moral difference, and even if you think it should make a legal difference when all else is equal, you should think it doesn't make a big enough difference to justify the state's imposing a significantly increased risk of harm on Alice when all else isn't equal. If it should be legal for Alice to have a hysterotomy abortion, you should agree that it should also be legal for her to have a dilation and curettage abortion, since that would be safer for her and no worse for Al. And if that's right, then you should reject the killing versus letting die objection.

But let's suppose my guess is wrong here and you think it would be okay for the state to prevent Shimp from choosing the safer disconnection method even though it would be wrong for the state to prevent him from being disconnected by the more dangerous method. If that's what you think, you should think it would be okay for the state to ban methods of abortion that kill the fetus before or during its removal but wrong for the state to ban methods like hysterotomy that involve removing the fetus and leaving it to die even if methods like hysterotomy are considerably more dangerous for the women who have abortions. As I mentioned earlier, saying some methods of abortion should be legal while others should be illegal amounts to a somewhat unusual position—one that won't fully satisfy people on either side of the abortion debate. But, as I also mentioned earlier, if that's what you end up thinking, you're still agreeing with the basic claim I'm trying to defend in this book. The claim that abortion should be legal doesn't have to mean every method of abortion should be legal. If you think it should be legal for Alice to have her pregnancy terminated prior to viability but only if it's done in some ways and not others, then you still think it should be legal for Alice to have an abortion prior to viability and so still agree with the basic claim I'm trying to defend in this book. No matter how much or how little you think the difference between killing and letting die ultimately matters, then, in the end the killing versus letting die objection gives you no reason to reject the basic claim I'm trying to defend in this book.

# 19

## Intentions

Freedonia is at war with Elbonia. Elbonia's losing. Its troops are running low on ammunition and low on morale. But they're still managing to inflict serious damage on the enemy, resulting in retaliation and heavy losses on both sides. Elbonia has one large ammunition plant left and it's still working. It's closely surrounded by housing for athletes who are there to train for the upcoming Olympics. They're the pride and joy of Elbonia. Meanwhile, two Freedonian bomber pilots have independently come to the same conclusion. They've each decided to drop a bomb on the ammunition plant. They've come to this conclusion for the same reason: dropping a bomb on the ammunition plant will hasten the end of the war and save many lives on both sides. But they've come to this reason in different ways.

The first bomber pilot is Fred. Here's how Fred sees things: "I want to force the enemy to surrender by reducing its already low ammunition supply. The best way to do this is to destroy as much of its ammunition as possible. And the most effective way to do that is to drop a bomb on its remaining ammunition plant. I realize that if I drop a bomb on the ammunition plant, the explosion will also kill a number of innocent civilians who live right next to it. And I feel really bad about that. But I'm not dropping the bomb in order to kill them. I'm dropping the bomb in order to destroy the ammunitions. The point of dropping the bomb is to destroy the ammunitions, not to kill the innocent civilians."

The second bomber pilot is Freddie. Here's how Freddie sees things: "I want to force the enemy to surrender by reducing its already low morale. The best way to do this is to kill as many of its most popular civilians as possible. And the most effective way to do that is to kill all the Olympic athletes living next to the ammunition plant. That's the most effective way to do it because those people are really popular and I can kill them all by blowing up the ammunition plant with a single bomb. This plan has an added bonus: it will also reduce the enemy's supply of ammunition. But that's just the icing on the cake. I'm not dropping the bomb in order to destroy the ammunitions. I'm dropping the bomb in order to kill the innocent civilians. The point of dropping the bomb is to kill the innocent civilians, not to destroy the ammunitions."

If you're like a lot of people, you'll think there's an important difference here between Fred and Freddie. Depending on the details of the story, you might approve of Fred's decision or you might not. But either way, if you're like a lot of people, you'll think what Freddie does is worse than what Fred does. Freddie's aim is to kill innocent civilians as a way of achieving his objective. But Fred doesn't aim to kill innocent civilians. In his case, the death of the civilians is what's sometimes called collateral damage. Philosophers often describe this difference by saying Freddie *intends* to bring about the death of the innocent civilians while Fred merely *foresees* that the innocent civilians will die. And a lot of people think this makes a difference. They think even if it's okay to do what Fred does, that doesn't mean it's okay to do what Freddie does. And they think this because even though the consequences are the same either way, the intentions are different.

If you're one of the people who responds to the case of Fred and Freddie in this way, you might think this poses yet another problem for my argument. That's because you might think the difference between Fred and Freddie is like a difference between Shimp and Alice. If you asked Shimp why he wanted to be disconnected from the bone marrow transferring machine, you might expect him to say something like this: "I want to be relieved of the burden of keeping McFall alive, and the only way to do that is to disconnect me from the machine. I realize that if I'm disconnected from the machine, McFall will die. And I feel really bad about that. But I'm not asking to be disconnected from the machine in order to bring about McFall's death. I'm asking to be disconnected in order to be relieved of the burden of keeping him alive. The point of disconnecting me is to relieve me of the burden of keeping McFall alive, not to bring about his death."

But you might expect that if you asked Alice why she wanted an abortion, she'd say something more like this: "I don't want to be a mother. The only way to make that happen is for Al to die, and the only way to make Al die is for me to have an abortion. Having an abortion also has an added bonus: it will relieve me of the burden of continuing to be pregnant for the next several months. But that's just the icing on the cake. I'm not asking to have an abortion in order to be relieved of the burden of several more months of pregnancy. I'm asking to have an abortion in order to bring about the death of Al. The point of having the abortion is to bring about Al's death, not to relieve me of the burden of several more months of pregnancy."

Now I'm not sure putting things this way is entirely fair to Alice. Maybe she wants Al dead. But maybe all she wants is to have Al removed from her body so she can be relieved of the burden of being pregnant. Maybe she feels bad about the fact that Al will die as a result of being removed from her body, just as Shimp feels bad about the fact that McFall will die as result of Shimp's being disconnected from the bone marrow transferring machine. And if that's why Alice wants to have an abortion, then the difference between intending to bring about a person's death and foreseeing that a person's death will be brought about isn't a difference between Shimp and Alice in the first place.

But let's go ahead and assume, at least for the sake of the argument, that Alice really does want the abortion because she wants Al dead. Avoiding several more months of pregnancy is just icing on the cake, as far as she's concerned. If that's right, and if you think what Freddie does is worse than what Fred does, you should also think what Alice does is worse than what Shimp does. And if you think what Alice does is worse than what Shimp does, then you don't have to think it would be wrong for the state to prevent Alice from having an abortion just because you think it would be wrong for the state to prevent Shimp from being disconnected from the bone marrow transferring machine. Again, my argument will seem to fall apart.

If you think my argument has fallen apart here because of the difference between intending and foreseeing, though, I think I can put it back together. Suppose Shimp really hated his cousin. Couldn't stand the sight of him. Suppose if you asked Shimp why he wanted to be disconnected from the bone marrow transferring machine, he'd say something like this: "I want McFall to die soon and the only way to make that happen is for me to be disconnected from the bone marrow transferring machine before he gets enough of my bone marrow. Disconnecting me from the machine will also have an added bonus: it will relieve me of the burden of continuing to have some of my bone marrow sucked out of me. But that's just the icing on the cake. I'm not asking to be disconnected from the machine in order to be relieved of the burden of having more bone marrow extracted from my body. I'm asking to be disconnected in order to bring about the death of McFall. The point of being disconnected is to bring about McFall's death, not to relieve me of the burden of having more bone marrow extracted."

If you think what Freddie does is worse than what Fred does, you'll think what Shimp does in this version of the story is worse than what Shimp does when all he wants is to be relieved of the burden of having his bone marrow removed. But the question isn't whether what Shimp does in this version of the story is worse, or whether what he does in this version is immoral. The question is whether it would be okay for the state to force Shimp to stay connected to the machine in this version. So let's focus on that question instead. Suppose Shimp demands to be disconnected from the machine and McFall's lawyer rushes over to the courthouse and says something like this to the Judge: "Your Honor, you have to force Mr. Shimp to let my client continue using his bone marrow because the only reason he wants to stop letting him use it is that he hates my client." Do you think the judge should go along with the lawyer's appeal in this case?

I'd be surprised if you did. If McFall had no right to use Shimp's bone marrow in the original case, why would McFall suddenly have this right simply because the only reason Shimp didn't want to let him have the bone marrow was that he hated him? It's not really that different from the versions of the story where Shimp decides not to help McFall because McFall is male or because McFall has Down syndrome. Just as in those cases, the reason Shimp has for refusing to keep McFall alive in this case may well lead you to think he's doing something morally worse. But also as in those cases, it's hard to believe you'll think this would be enough to make it okay for the state to force Shimp to let McFall continue using the bone marrow. And if you don't think that, you'll have to say the same thing about the case of Al and Alice even if Alice really does want the abortion just because she wants Al to be dead. That may be enough to make what Alice does worse than it would be if she simply wanted to be relieved of the burden of pregnancy. But if it's not enough to make it okay for the state to prevent Shimp from being disconnected from the bone marrow transferring machine, it can't be enough to make it okay for the state to prevent Alice from having an abortion. So the difference between intending and foreseeing may make some difference. But in the end, it doesn't make enough of a difference to undermine my argument.

## 20

# Other Differences

I can think of two more differences between Shimp's situation and Alice's situation that might seem to matter. If you can think of further differences, you should test them the same way I've been testing the ones I've thought of here: come up with your own version of the story of McFall and Shimp that makes Shimp's situation like Alice's situation in terms of whatever difference you have in mind and then ask yourself whether you think it would be okay for the state to force Shimp to let McFall use his bone marrow in that version of the story. If you think it would still be wrong for the state to force Shimp to let McFall use his bone marrow even after you've made Shimp's situation like Alice's situation in terms of whatever difference you have in mind, then as far as you're concerned, that difference doesn't really make a difference. If it would still be wrong for the state to force Shimp to let McFall use his bone marrow even if Shimp's situation were just like Alice's in that particular respect, then the fact that Alice's situation is like that in that particular respect can't be enough to make it okay for the state to force Alice to let Al use her uterus. But if you think it would be okay for the state to force Shimp to let McFall use his bone marrow in your new version of the story, and if you're convinced that your new version of the story makes Shimp's situation like Alice's situation in some particular respect, then you'll be entitled to conclude that the fact that Alice's situation is like that in that particular respect really is enough to make it okay for the state to force Alice to carry her pregnancy to term.

My guess is you aren't going to find a difference I've overlooked that will make a difference to you in this way if you construct the cases carefully. You may have noticed that McFall is sick while Al is healthy, for example, and I haven't discussed this difference between the cases, but I doubt you'll think that healthy people have a right to use other people's bodies when they need them while sick people don't. If I'm right about that, then this difference won't pose a problem for my argument, either. It's still worth your considering whether there are further differences I haven't thought of, of course, but in the meantime, let me say a few things about the other two differences I have thought of. I'm not going to say too much about them, though, because even if they do make a difference, they do it by making my argument stronger, not weaker.

The first difference has to do with the burdens Shimp would have to endure in order to keep McFall alive and the burdens Alice would have to endure in order to keep Al alive. Shimp would have to have some bone marrow extracted from his body. Alice would have to carry an unwanted pregnancy to term. Let's say Alice is eight or nine weeks pregnant right now. Most abortions take place by around then. And let's say her pregnancy is about average in terms of the various physical effects pregnancies tend to have on women. So to keep Al alive, Alice would have to spend the next seven months or so enduring all the burdens of a typical pregnancy and then give birth to Al. There's a pretty big difference between having some bone marrow removed from your body and being pregnant for seven months and then giving birth. And it's not just that the burdens in the two cases are different. It's that the burdens in one case seem quite a bit greater than the burdens in the other case. That might seem to make a difference.

I'm not a doctor, but from what I can tell, donating bone marrow typically involves checking into a hospital in the morning, having a surgical procedure done a few hours later, and checking out toward the end of the day or the following morning. In the vast majority of cases, the donor is given general anesthesia, though in some cases local anesthesia is used instead. The doctors typically use specially designed needles to remove the marrow from two areas toward the back of the pelvic bone. The incisions are so small that they don't require stitches. Since anesthesia is used, the donor feels no pain during this process. Most donors do experience some discomfort and side effects after the procedure, though. The most common include fatigue, back or hip pain, muscle pain, headaches, and bruising where the incisions were made. The aches and pains might last a few days, but they could last as long as several weeks. Some donors say it feels like having achy hip bones or a muscle sprain in the back. Others say it feels like you fell on your butt. Most donors are back to their regular routines in a few days and feel fully recovered within a few weeks.

I'm also not a woman, let alone a woman who's carried a pregnancy to term. But from what I can tell, being forced to endure the final seven months of a typical pregnancy and give birth to a child sounds quite a bit more burdensome than being forced to donate some bone marrow. There are the common physical symptoms like fatigue, nausea, vomiting, heartburn, indigestion, headaches, cramps, and body aches. There's the weight gain and the discomfort and difficulty of moving around that goes along with it and there are the negative long-term health consequences if the added weight isn't taken off later. There are the hormone changes and their effects, things like irritability, mood swings, and anxiety, and sometimes a period of depression after it's all over. And, of course, there's the pain of childbirth itself, which many women describe as the most excruciating pain they've ever experienced. It certainly sounds a lot more painful than how it feels when you fall on your butt. And needless to say, most women do not deliver while they are under general anesthesia, and they are not back to their regular routines just a few days after they give birth. The recovery period seems to be longer and harder, too. So all in all, it sounds like the burden the state would impose on Alice by forcing her to keep Al alive would be considerably greater than the burden it would impose on Shimp by forcing him to keep McFall alive. I'm guessing if you had to choose between being forced to donate some bone marrow and being forced to spend the next seven months carrying an unwanted pregnancy to term, you'd have a pretty strong preference for going the bone marrow route.

Let's assume that's true. What kind of difference would it make to my argument? We can answer this question by changing the case of McFall and Shimp yet again. So suppose David Shimp had actually been Diana Shimp and the only way McFall was going to survive required her to have an embryo implanted in her uterus and to gestate it for seven months before giving birth to the resulting child. Maybe for some reason harvesting stem cells from the umbilical cord at that point would be the only way to cure McFall's condition. Would it be okay for the state to force Diana Shimp to do this in that case? If you agreed it would wrong for the state to force David Shimp to let McFall use some of his bone marrow, I assume you'll agree it would also be wrong for the state to force Diana Shimp to have an embryo implanted in her uterus and gestate it for seven months. But you'll probably think more than this. You'll probably think it would be even more wrong for the state to do this to Diana Shimp than it would be to force David Shimp to donate some bone marrow. How much more wrong? That depends on how much greater you think the burden would be. I'm guessing you'll say the burden would be much greater. If I'm right about that, then not only should you think it's wrong for the state to force Alice to carry her pregnancy to term but you should also think it would be more wrong for the state to do this to Alice than it would be for the state to force David Shimp to let McFall have some of his bone marrow. Probably a lot more wrong.

I've been assuming all along you agree it would have been wrong for the state to force Shimp to let McFall use some of his bone marrow. But I haven't really asked you how wrong you think it would have been. So let me ask you to think about that now. My guess is you're going to say it would have been pretty seriously wrong. I wouldn't be surprised if you said it would be outrageous. That's certainly what Judge Flaherty thought. If I'm right about that, then even if the difference between the burdens involved in donating bone marrow and the burdens involved in carrying a pregnancy to term doesn't make a difference, you should still think it wouldn't just be wrong for the state to prevent Alice from having an abortion. You should think it would be pretty seriously wrong, maybe outrageously wrong. But I'm guessing you think the difference between the burdens involved in donating bone marrow and the burdens involved in carrying a pregnancy to term does make a difference. If I'm right about that, you should think it wouldn't just be seriously wrong, or even outrageously wrong, for the state to prevent Alice from having an abortion. You should think it would be even more wrong than that. Probably a lot more wrong than that.

Before I move on to the other difference I have in mind, let me make one more comment about this one. At a number of points so far I've emphasized that my defense of the claim that abortion should be legal doesn't depend on rejecting the claim that abortion is immoral. As long as you think it would be wrong for the state to force Shimp to let McFall use his bone marrow, it doesn't matter whether you think it was immoral for Shimp to refuse to let McFall use it. Either way, what you think is enough to show that abortion should be legal. This is an important feature of my argument, but it can also lead to an important confusion. That's because if you think it was immoral for Shimp to refuse to let McFall use his bone marrow, you might think my argument commits you to saying it would be immoral for Alice to refuse to let Al use her uterus.

But this first difference between the two cases shows that my argument doesn't have this implication. If you think it was immoral for Shimp not to let McFall use his bone marrow, it's probably because you think the burden involved in donating bone marrow isn't really that great. But even if you think this, you'll probably agree that the burden involved in carrying an unwanted pregnancy to term is far greater. As a result, even if you think it was immoral for Shimp not to let McFall use his bone marrow, you may well say something different about the version of the story where Diana Shimp would have to have an embryo implanted in her and carry the pregnancy to term in order to save McFall's life. In that version of the story, you may very well say that while it would be incredibly generous for Shimp to suffer such a significant burden in order to save McFall's life, it wouldn't be immoral for her to decline to do so. If that's what you say, then you should say the same thing about Alice: it would be incredibly generous for her to carry her pregnancy to term in order to save Al's life, but it wouldn't be immoral for her to decline to do so. So while it's important to see that you can accept my defense of the claim that abortion should be legal even if you think it would be immoral for Alice to have an abortion, it's also important to see that nothing about my argument supports the claim that abortion is immoral.

Let's now move on to the other difference between Shimp and Alice that I had in mind: Pretty much anyone can donate bone marrow, but only women can carry a pregnancy to term. So if the law said you have to donate bone marrow whenever that would keep someone alive, the burdens imposed by the law would be distributed more or less evenly across society. But if the law said you have to carry a pregnancy to term whenever that would keep someone alive, the burdens imposed by the law would fall entirely on women. Laws prohibiting abortion don't just impose bigger burdens than laws requiring bone marrow donation. They also impose burdens less equally.

This difference might make a difference, too. For one thing, women as a group have historically been disadvantaged in a variety of ways relative to men, and they continue to be disadvantaged in a variety of ways relative to men. This might make it worse for a state to impose a burden exclusively on women than it would be to impose the same degree of burden on everyone. There's also a common belief that nurturing is more of a girl thing than a guy thing. So if the law forces women to let other people use their bodies as a form of life support but doesn't force men to let other people use their bodies as a form of life support, it would seem to reinforce a pernicious gender stereotype. That might make it even worse for a state to impose this particular kind of burden exclusively on women than it would be to impose other kinds of burdens exclusively on women.

If you're wondering whether this difference really does make a difference, you should think once more about McFall and Shimp. Suppose whenever people were diagnosed with aplastic anemia they died if someone didn't let them have some of their bone marrow. Suppose while in some cases people freely chose to donate the bone marrow they needed, in other cases they didn't. And suppose in response to this situation that the government passed a law forcing people to donate the needed bone marrow in such cases. If you agree with Judge Flaherty's decision in the real case of *McFall v. Shimp*, you'll presumably think it would be wrong for the state to do this. But now suppose for some reason only women were capable of donating bone marrow. Men and women could each be saved by receiving donated bone marrow, but only women could save people by donating it. Maybe something about male bone marrow made it useless once it was removed from a man's body.

Do you think it would be even worse for the government to force people to donate bone marrow in that case? My guess is you'll think if only women were able to give bone marrow it would be at least a bit worse for a state to force people to give bone marrow than it would be if anyone could give bone marrow. You might well think it would be more than just a bit worse. Maybe a whole lot worse. If I'm right about that, you should again think a law forcing women to carry their pregnancies to term would be even more objectionable than a law forcing people to donate bone marrow. Maybe just a bit more objectionable. But maybe a whole lot more objectionable. And even if you don't think it would make a difference if only women were capable of donating bone marrow, you should still think laws against abortion are pretty seriously wrong as long as you think laws forcing people to give bone marrow would be not just wrong but also pretty seriously wrong. So either way, this second difference between Shimp and Alice can't weaken my case for abortion rights, either. As with the first difference, it can only strengthen it.

# 21

## Other Objections

Two final objections to my argument maintain that I've been misleading you in one way or another. The first points out that every time I've presented you with a version of the story of McFall and Shimp, I've asked whether you think it would be okay for the state to force Shimp to let McFall use his bone marrow in that case. I've then said if you don't think the facts about that version of the story would make it okay for the state to do that, you shouldn't think the same facts about a pregnant woman and her fetus would be enough to make it okay for the state to force the woman to carry her pregnancy to term. The assumption behind all this has been that if the state bans abortion, it forces a woman to carry her pregnancy to term. So if it would be wrong for the state to force a woman to carry her pregnancy to term, it would be wrong for the state to ban abortion.

But some people who consider themselves pro-life might question this assumption. They think abortion should be illegal, but in thinking this, they may not see themselves as endorsing the idea that agents of the state should literally lay hands on a pregnant woman's body and force her to continue gestating her fetus. If that's right, then they might say something like this: the claim that it would be wrong for the state to force Shimp to let McFall use his bone marrow doesn't show that it would be wrong for the state to make it illegal for the pregnant woman to have an abortion. It just shows that it would be wrong for the state to literally force the woman to continue gestating the fetus. And that, they might think, is another matter.

I don't think you should accept this objection for two reasons. First, I don't think you should accept the claim that there's a difference between the state's forcing you to do something and the state's saying it's illegal for you not to do it. I bet you think the state forces you to pay taxes, for example, even if agents of the state don't literally grab your hand and force you to fill out the forms. Banning abortion forces women to carry their pregnancies to term in the same way banning anything forces people not to do that thing. But second, and perhaps more importantly, even if you do think there's a difference here, I don't think you should think the difference matters. And, yes, once again, I think the case of McFall and Shimp can help us see this.

It's true that each time I gave you a version of that story, I asked if you thought it would be okay for the state to force Shimp to give McFall the bone marrow he needed. But suppose I had instead asked a different question: Do you think it would be okay for the state to make it illegal for Shimp not to give McFall the bone marrow? Do you think you would have given a different answer? That's hard to believe. If you don't think it would be okay for the state to force Shimp to let McFall use his bone marrow, it's got to be because you think McFall didn't have the right to use Shimp's bone marrow. And if McFall didn't have the right to use Shimp's bone marrow, why would it be okay for the state to make it illegal for Shimp not to give it to him? So I think this first objection can safely be set aside.

The second objection complains about a different way that my presentation here may have been misleading. I've tried to address a variety of differences between the case of McFall and Shimp and the case of a fetus and a pregnant woman, but I've talked about each difference one at a time. So I've said things like "if this particular feature of Shimp's situation wouldn't be enough to make it okay for the state to force Shimp to let McFall use his bone marrow, then this particular feature of a pregnant woman's situation can't be enough to make it okay for the state to force her to carry her pregnancy to term." But this approach might be hiding a problem with my argument. Maybe no one difference between the two cases is enough to make a difference, but some combination of differences is enough to make a difference. If some combination of differences between the case of McFall and Shimp and the case Al and Alice makes a difference, then you can still agree that it would be wrong for the state to force Shimp to let McFall use his bone marrow without having to agree that it would be wrong for the state to force Alice to let Al use her uterus.

I can't rule out this possibility, but it strikes me as unlikely. If you think there's a problem for my argument here, though, you can test your hypothesis by coming up with your own version of the story of McFall and Shimp—one that makes Shimp's situation like Alice's situation in terms of whatever combination of differences you have in mind. And you can then ask yourself whether you think it would be okay for the state to force Shimp to let McFall use his bone marrow in your version of the story. If you agree with me that the difference between cousin and son by itself doesn't make a difference and that the difference between intending and foreseeing by itself doesn't make a difference, for example, you could come up with a version of the story where someone stole sperm from Shimp to create McFall and where the reason Shimp wants be disconnected from the bone marrow transferring machine is that he doesn't like the idea of McFall continuing to exist. That would be a case where McFall is Shimp's son in the same way Al is Alice's son and where Shimp's intentions are the same as Alice's intentions. If you had two other differences in mind, you could come up with a version of the story that changes things in terms of both of them so that the case of McFall and Shimp would be just like the case of Al and Alice in both respects. Or you could combine more than two differences.

If you think it would still be wrong for the state to force Shimp to let McFall use his bone marrow even after you've made Shimp's situation like Alice's situation in terms of whatever combination of differences you have in mind, then as far as you're concerned that combination of differences doesn't really make a difference. If it would still be wrong for the state to force Shimp to let McFall use his bone marrow even if Shimp's situation were just like Alice's in terms of some given combination of features, then the fact that Alice's situation has that particular combination of features can't be enough to make it okay for the state to force Alice to let Al use her uterus. But if you think it would be okay for the state to force Shimp to let McFall use his bone marrow in the new version of the story, and if you're convinced that the new version of the story makes Shimp's situation like Alice's situation in terms of some particular combination of features, then you'll be entitled to conclude that the fact that Alice's situation is like that in terms of that particular combination of features is enough to make it okay for the state to force Alice to carry her pregnancy to term. And, again, the same would go for the case of Barbara and Bob.

My guess, as before, is that you aren't going to find a combination of differences that makes a difference to you in this way if you construct the cases carefully. Combining one irrelevant difference with another irrelevant difference is just going to result in a bigger irrelevant difference. Adding yet another irrelevant difference is just going to make the difference bigger, not more relevant. But, again, I could be wrong. If I've convinced you that none of the differences between Alice and Shimp makes a difference individually, you should certainly explore this possibility before reaching a final conclusion about my argument. But I'm not going to take the time to explore it here. Instead, I want to move on from the question of laws that prohibit abortion to the question of laws that permit but restrict it.

**PART III**

# WHY ABORTION SHOULD BE LESS RESTRICTED

# 22

## Insurance Restrictions

Let's now suppose you've thought through all the objections I've considered, as well as any additional objections you might have thought of on your own. And let's also suppose, quite optimistically I admit, that you've been convinced by what I've said. You think Judge Flaherty made the right call in *McFall v. Shimp*, and you agree that the lesson we can draw from that case shows that abortion should be legal. Even if you agree that abortion should be legal, that doesn't mean you have to think the government shouldn't try to make it harder for women to get abortions. It doesn't even mean you have to think the government shouldn't restrict access to abortion in various ways. It's legal to buy cigarettes, after all, but it seems fine for the government to try to make it harder for people to buy cigarettes and to restrict their sale and use in various ways. So even if abortion should be legal, that by itself doesn't mean it would be wrong for the government to try to make it harder for women to get abortions or to restrict access to abortion in various ways. Indeed, if we continue to assume that every fetus is a person with a right to life, it might seem reasonable to conclude that the government should do a great deal to make it harder for women to have abortions and a great deal to restrict access to them. But I think this, too, turns out to be a mistake. If the argument I offered in part I is successful, then not only should abortion be legal even if every fetus is a person but even if every fetus is a person, abortion should be much less restricted than it currently is. And once again, I think the story of McFall and Shimp can help us to see this. So for the purposes of this final part of the book, I'm now going to assume, at least for the sake of the argument, that you've been convinced by what I've said so far. And I'm going to try to convince you that if this is so, then many current legal restrictions on abortion are morally unacceptable even if every fetus is a person with a right to life.

One way to make it harder for women to have abortions is to make abortions more expensive. And one way to make abortions more expensive is to prevent women from buying insurance that would pay for them. Consider the case of Alice again, the pregnant young software engineer from St. Louis. Alice has a good job now, but what I didn't mention before is that she just started working there a few weeks ago. Her bank account is pretty much empty at the moment, she has big student loans to pay off and significant credit card debt, and she's currently behind on her rent. Alice has decent health insurance through her employer, and the insurance will cover the costs of prenatal care and childbirth. But if she decides to have an abortion, the insurance won't pay for that. The clinic she went to says an abortion would cost her about $1,000, and Alice doesn't have that kind of money right now.

If the insurance Alice gets from her job had included abortion coverage, the insurance would have cost the company a bit more to purchase, and they might have deducted a little bit more from Alice's paycheck each month as a result. Still, Alice could have afforded the slight increase in her insurance costs. What she can't afford is to pay $1,000 for an abortion right now. Alice's employer would have been happy to offer a comprehensive health insurance plan that included abortion coverage. The reason they didn't is simple: it's illegal in the state of Missouri for an employer to offer a comprehensive health insurance plan that includes abortion coverage unless the insurance only covers abortion in cases where the woman's life is endangered. In fact, not only is it illegal for an employer to offer an employee such a plan in that state but it's also illegal for an individual to purchase such a plan in that state on their own. And a number of other states have similar laws. If we assume that Al, the fetus gestating in Alice's uterus, is a person with a right to life, is it okay for the state to try to discourage Alice from having an abortion in this way?

Well, let's see how we'd answer the same kind of question in the case of McFall and Shimp. To figure that out, we'd have to start by coming up with a version of that story that fits Alice's circumstances. So let's suppose Shimp is just as poor as Alice is, that it would cost Shimp $1,000 to be disconnected from the bone marrow transferring machine, and that while Shimp's health insurance will cover the costs of his staying in the hospital until McFall has gotten all the bone marrow he needs, it won't cover the costs of unplugging Shimp before then. And let's assume that Shimp's employer would have been happy to offer Shimp a comprehensive health insurance plan that included the costs of being disconnected from the machine and that his employer didn't do that only because offering such an insurance plan was illegal. This seems to give us just the kind of story we need to answer the question about Alice's insurance. Al doesn't have the right to use Alice's uterus, but she can't afford to prevent him from using her uterus. McFall doesn't have the right to use Shimp's bone marrow, but Shimp can't afford to prevent him from using his bone marrow. In each case, the reason they can't afford to prevent the other person from using their body is that their health insurance won't cover the costs. And in each case their health insurance won't cover the costs only because the state made it illegal for it to cover the costs.

Assuming this is the right version of the story of McFall and Shimp to consider, what should we say about it? Here's what

I think you should say if you agree that McFall doesn't have the right to use Shimp's bone marrow. First, if Shimp did have $1,000 to cover the costs of being disconnected from the bone marrow transferring machine, it would be wrong for the state to steal that $1,000 from him to prevent him from being able to afford to be disconnected from it. If you think it would be wrong for the state to prevent Shimp from being disconnected from the machine, it's hard to see how you could think it would be okay for the state to steal the money from Shimp that he'd need to use to pay to be disconnected from it. Stealing the $1,000 from him in this case would prevent him from being disconnected. So if it would be wrong for the state to prevent him from being disconnected, it would be wrong for the state to steal the $1,000 from him to prevent him from being disconnected.

Second, if it would be wrong for the state to steal the $1,000 from Shimp if Shimp already had the $1,000, then it would be wrong for the state to prevent someone from giving Shimp the $1,000 if Shimp didn't already have the $1,000. Suppose a friend of Shimp's offered to give him the money to cover the costs of being disconnected from the machine. Preventing the friend from giving Shimp the money would prevent Shimp from being disconnected from the machine just as surely as stealing the money from Shimp if he already had the money would prevent Shimp from being disconnected from it. So if you agree it would be wrong for the state to steal the $1,000 from Shimp if he already had it, you should agree it would also be wrong for the state to prevent someone from giving McFall the $1,000 if he didn't already have it.

Finally, if it would be wrong for the state to prevent someone from giving Shimp the $1,000 to pay to be disconnected from the bone marrow transferring machine, it would be wrong for the state to prevent someone from giving Shimp something else that Shimp could use to pay to be disconnected from it, like a coupon worth $1,000 at the hospital or a health insurance policy that would cover the bill. Preventing someone from giving Shimp money to use to pay the bill is no different from preventing someone from giving Shimp a coupon or an insurance policy to use to pay the bill. So if it would be wrong for the state to prevent someone from giving Shimp the money to pay the bill, it would be wrong for the state to prevent someone from giving Shimp a health insurance policy that would pay the bill, too. And if all of this is true, then if it would be wrong for the state to prevent Shimp from disconnecting himself from the machine, it would be wrong for the state to prevent someone from giving Shimp a health insurance policy that would pay the costs of his being disconnected from the machine. Assuming you agree it would be wrong for the state to prevent Shimp from being disconnected from the machine, you should agree it would be wrong for the state to prevent Shimp's employer from giving him a health insurance policy that would cover the costs of his being disconnected from it.

But if that's what you think about this version of the story of McFall and Shimp, you should think the same thing about this version of the case of Al and Alice. If it would be wrong for the state to prevent Alice from having an abortion because Al doesn't have the right to use Alice's uterus, then it would be wrong for the state to steal $1,000 from Alice to prevent her from having an abortion. If that would be wrong, it would be wrong for the state to prevent someone from giving Alice $1,000 to pay for the abortion. And if that would be wrong, it would be wrong for the state to prevent someone from giving Alice a health insurance policy that would pay for the abortion. So if it would be wrong for the state to prevent Alice from having an abortion, it would be wrong for the state to make it illegal for her employer to give her a health insurance policy that would pay for the abortion. And since that's what you think in the case of McFall and Shimp even though McFall was a person with a right to life, that's what you should think about the case of Al and Alice even if you think Al is a person with a right to life. If every fetus is a person with a right to life, that might turn out to justify some restrictions on abortion, but it won't justify laws that prevent women from being offered comprehensive health insurance plans that cover the costs of abortion.

Before moving on to consider other kinds of abortion restrictions, let me address a few complications about what I've said about this kind. First, I focused on a case where a woman was too poor to pay for an abortion on her own. In that kind of case, when the state prevents her employer from offering health insurance that covers abortion, the state prevents her from having an abortion. So if it's wrong for the state to prevent her from having an abortion, it's wrong for the state to prevent her employer from offering such insurance. But what about women who can easily afford to pay for their own abortions? Does my argument apply to them, too? I think it does. Suppose Shimp actually had plenty of money in the bank and had no unpaid bills or loans. But suppose a friend of his wanted to give him $1,000 to cover the cost of his being disconnected from the bone marrow transferring machine anyway. It still seems wrong for the state to steal this money from Shimp after his friend gives it to him or to prevent his friend from giving Shimp the money in the first place. Even though doing so wouldn't prevent Shimp from being disconnected from the machine, it would still make it harder for him to do so by preventing someone else from paying for it. And if Shimp really has the right to be disconnected from the machine, it's hard to see what would justify this restriction. If that's right, then it would be wrong to prevent Shimp's employer from offering him comprehensive health insurance that would cover the costs of being disconnected from the machine even if Shimp had plenty of extra money. And if that's right, we should say the same thing about Alice. Even if Alice had plenty of money in the bank and had no unpaid bills or loans, it would still be wrong for the state to prevent a friend of hers from giving her $1,000 to cover the cost of an abortion and so it would be wrong for the state to prevent her employer from offering her comprehensive health insurance that would cover those costs.

A second complication has to do with the fact that I've focused on the case of Alice here and Alice was raped. What about women who get pregnant as a result of contraceptive failure or because they failed to use contraception? Does my argument apply to them, too? Again, I think it does. The argument depends on the claim that if Shimp would have the right to be disconnected from the bone marrow transferring machine, it would be wrong for the state to prevent his employer from offering him a health insurance policy that would cover the cost of disconnecting him from it. But as we saw when we looked at the consent objection and the responsibility objection, if Shimp has the right to be disconnected from the machine in the version of the story where he's kidnapped and plugged into it, he also has the right to be disconnected from the machine in the versions of the story where he ends up plugged into it because he freely chose to walk across the hospital room and slipped and fell onto it, regardless of whether he decided to wear the special nonslip shoes. If that's right, then it would be wrong for the state to prevent Shimp from being offered health insurance that would cover the cost of his being disconnected from the machine in those versions of the story, too.

And if that's right, then the argument I've offered here also shows that it would be wrong for the state to prevent Barbara from being offered health insurance that would cover the cost of her abortion when she got pregnant because of contraceptive failure and wrong to prevent Carol from being offered health insurance that would cover the cost of her abortion when she got pregnant because she didn't feel like using birth control. And the same would go for every case where it should be legal for a woman to have an abortion. If it would be wrong for the state to prevent Shimp from unplugging himself from the machine in the case where he does so because of McFall's sex or because McFall has Down syndrome, for example, then it would be wrong for the state to prevent Dorothy from being offered health insurance that would cover the cost of the abortion she wants because Daniel is male and wrong for the state to prevent Elaine from being offered health insurance that would cover the cost of the abortion she wants because Evan has Down syndrome. If it would be wrong for the state to prevent Alice from being offered health insurance that covers the abortion she wants, then it would be wrong for the state to prevent a woman from being offered health insurance that covers abortion under all the circumstances in which the abortion should be legal.

# 23

## The Hyde Amendment

One way a state can make it harder for women to get abortions is by preventing insurance companies from covering the costs of an abortion as part of a comprehensive health insurance policy. Another way a state can do this is by refusing to cover the costs itself. Consider, for example, the case of Henry Hyde. Hyde was a Republican congressman from Illinois and a major opponent of abortion. In 1976, he sponsored an addition to a spending bill. His goal was to ban the use of federal funds to pay for abortions. The amendment passed and became something of an annual tradition. It's come to be known as the Hyde Amendment.

The wording of the Hyde Amendment has changed somewhat over the years, but the core idea has remained the same: when funds are allocated to the Department of Health and Human Services, they come with a string attached, courtesy of the U.S. Congress. The string says that none of the money can be used to pay for abortions, or to pay for health insurance that covers abortions, except in extreme cases like life-threatening pregnancies. Its biggest effect has been on Medicaid, the main federal health insurance program for low-income people. As a result of the Hyde Amendment, poor women who get their health coverage through Medicaid can only have the costs of an abortion covered in the most extreme circumstances. Over the years, Congress has also passed a number of similar laws that prevent federal funds from being used to pay for abortions in other contexts. And a number of states have passed similar laws imposing restrictions on how their money is spent. What should we say about all this?

Well, what would we say in the case of McFall and Shimp? Suppose a number of people were diagnosed with aplastic anemia each year and that each of them would die if someone didn't let them have some of their bone marrow. And suppose each year a number of people found themselves connected to a bone marrow transferring machine that was starting to give some of their bone marrow to one of these aplastic anemia victims. In some cases, people were kidnapped and woke up connected to the machines; in other cases, they slipped and fell onto the machines as they walked across a slippery floor; and in still others, they freely chose to connect themselves to the machine, thinking at the time that they'd be willing to stay connected for as long as it took to get the job done. But suppose while some of these people were willing to stay connected to the machines once they found themselves connected to them in these various ways, others were not. If you agreed with Judge Flaherty's decision in the real case of *McFall v. Shimp*, you'll presumably agree that these people should be free to disconnect themselves if they want to. If it would be wrong for the state to force one person to let another person use their bone marrow, it would be wrong for the state to force more than one person to let another person use their bone marrow.

But now let's add another twist. Let's suppose it costs $1,000 to be unplugged from the machine. Suppose at first the government agrees to cover this cost for anyone who's eligible for Medicaid. But suppose a member of Congress, Representative Jekyll, then has the following idea: we could probably save the lives of some people with aplastic anemia by banning the use of federal funds to pay for the costs of unplugging people from bone marrow transferring machines. People who can afford it will still get themselves unplugged if they want to, but at least this way we could use the bodies of poor people as a source of bone marrow and save some lives.

Strictly speaking, agreeing with Judge Flaherty's decision in the real case of *McFall v. Shimp* doesn't commit you to rejecting Congressman Jekyll's idea. If you agree with Judge Flaherty, you agree it would be wrong for the state to force people to let others use their bone marrow. But just because it would be wrong for the state to force people to let others use their bone marrow, that doesn't mean it would be wrong for the state to refuse to help people avoid letting others use their bone marrow. The claim that the government should let you be free not to do something doesn't mean the government should have to pay to help you avoid doing it. So the mere fact that you agree with Judge Flaherty's decision in the real case of *McFall v. Shimp* doesn't mean you have to disagree with Congressman Jekyll's proposal about what to do in this imaginary version of the story.

Still, even if your view about the real case of McFall and Shimp doesn't force your hand here, I find it hard to believe you'll be on board with the idea that the state should deprive poor people of the health insurance coverage it would otherwise give them just so it could use their bone marrow to keep other people alive. My guess is you'll find that idea pretty grotesque. If I'm right about that, you should say the same thing about the Hyde Amendment. And, more importantly, you should say the same thing about the Hyde Amendment even if you think every fetus is a person with a right to life. Either depriving poor people of the health insurance they would otherwise receive so their bodies can be used to keep other people alive is okay or it isn't. If it isn't okay in the case where they are deprived of the health insurance they would otherwise receive so their bone marrow can be used to keep other people alive, I can't see why it would be okay in the case where they are deprived of the health insurance they would otherwise receive so their uteruses can be used to keep other people alive.

I can think of a few objections you might have at this point, though. You might object, for example, that many people oppose abortion on religious grounds, and you might think it would be wrong for the state to use their tax money to pay for abortions because of this. But Christian Scientists oppose bone marrow transfusions on religious grounds. And both they and Jehovah's Witnesses oppose blood transfusions on religious grounds. Do you think it's wrong for Medicaid to cover the costs of blood and bone marrow transfusions because of taxpayers who oppose them on religious grounds? I doubt it. And if you don't, you can't say it's wrong for Medicaid to cover the costs of abortion because of taxpayers who oppose abortion on religious grounds.

Or maybe you favor a more modest role for the government as a general matter. You think the only legitimate use of tax money is to pay for a police force, judicial system, and national defense. In that case, you'll object to Medicaid paying for abortions because you'll object to Medicaid paying for anything. You'll think helping poor people afford health care should be left to private charities, not public funds. If you think the ideal state would be a minimal state of this sort, you should think an ideal state wouldn't use tax money to fund Medicaid at all. But that doesn't mean you should think it would be wrong for the state to include abortion coverage as a part of Medicaid given that the state does, in fact, fund Medicaid. That's because in the world we actually live in, the state will almost certainly end up spending even more tax money in ways you'll consider unjustified if it doesn't do this. This might be true only because the government spends a lot of tax money helping the children of poor people in ways you think it shouldn't, but that doesn't make it any less true. So if your concern is about the state spending tax money on services beyond what an ideal minimal state would provide, not only should you think it would be okay for Medicaid to include abortion coverage given that Medicaid exists but you should also think it really ought to do so given that Medicaid exists.

Finally, you might think Medicaid shouldn't pay for abortions because you might think having an abortion isn't really a health issue in the first place. Or, at least, you might think it's only a health issue in the kinds of extreme cases where exceptions to the Hyde Amendment already allow Medicaid to be used anyhow. Having a tumor means you're unhealthy, you might say, so it's fair to expect your health coverage to pay to have a tumor removed. But being pregnant doesn't mean you're unhealthy. It just means you're pregnant. So there's no reason to expect your health insurance to pay to have the fetus removed. If that's right, then the Hyde Amendment makes good sense after all.

There might be something to this objection. But I don't think there's enough. And I think McFall and Shimp can help us see this. Suppose Shimp couldn't afford to pay the costs involved in being disconnected from the bone marrow transferring machine and someone said Medicaid shouldn't cover the costs of disconnecting him because being stuck to a bone marrow transferring machine isn't really a health issue. It's not like having a tumor or a disease. How would we respond to them? I think we'd say something like this: if you were impaled by a sharp object and as a result some of your bone marrow was slowly leaking out, it would clearly be a health issue and the kind of thing your health insurance should pay to address. If the leaking bone marrow happened to be used to keep someone else alive, that wouldn't change the fact that it was a health issue for you. If that sounds like the right kind of response to you, you should say the same thing about pregnancy. If a condition caused a woman to have all the physical symptoms of pregnancy but didn't involve her body's keeping another person alive, the effects on her body would clearly pose a health issue for her and be the kind of thing her health insurance should pay to address. The fact that when all these symptoms are caused by pregnancy, they are caused by her body's keeping another person alive doesn't change the fact that the symptoms themselves pose a health issue for her. So this, too, doesn't seem like a good reason to support the Hyde Amendment.

If you agree it would be wrong to deprive poor people of the health insurance they would otherwise receive so we could use their bone marrow to keep other people alive, then you should agree that it's wrong to deprive poor women of the health insurance they would otherwise receive so we can use their uteruses to keep other people alive. My guess is you'll agree it would be wrong to deprive poor people of health insurance so we could use their bone marrow to keep other people alive. You would be against the Jekyll Amendment. And if you'd be against the Jekyll Amendment, you should be against the Hyde Amendment, too.

# 24

## Mandatory Waiting Periods

One way you can make it harder for women to get abortions is by making abortions more expensive. Here's another way: you can make them wait. There are two ways a state can do this. First, it can impose a limit on how quickly an abortion can be scheduled. Every state requires a patient to give informed consent before they receive medical attention. So one thing a state can do is tell a woman she can't give informed consent to having an abortion until she's received the appropriate counseling and then say she can't have an abortion until a certain amount of time has passed after she's had the counseling. Thirty-five states currently do this. The required waiting periods range from 24 to 72 hours. In South Dakota, a woman can be forced to wait even longer because the 72-hour waiting period there doesn't count weekends and state holidays. Another thing a state can do is impose additional requirements a woman has to meet before she can get the abortion. Some states, for example, require women who want abortions to get an ultrasound first. Is it okay for states to force women to wait before they get an abortion in these ways?

How we answer this question may depend on how these waiting periods discourage women from having abortions. One way they work is by making abortions more expensive. Many of the states that require abortion counseling, for example, require it to take place in person at the clinic. Since the woman has to wait at least 24 hours after this before going back for her abortion, this means she has to visit the clinic on two different days. If she doesn't live close enough to the clinic, this means she'll have to spend at least one night away from home. That can mean meals out, a hotel room, and lost wages. If she has children, it can also mean added child-care costs. And many abortion clinics are only open a few days a week. So requiring a woman who comes in on a Monday to wait 24 hours before coming back may in effect mean she can't come back until Wednesday or Thursday. Even if she lives close enough to get to the clinic and back in a day, requiring her to make two separate visits still effectively doubles the amount she'll have to spend on gas and increases the time she may have to take off from work or find someone to watch her kids. Two appointments at the clinic will also cost more than one, and if she has to undergo an ultrasound, that will probably cost her at least few hundred dollars more.

If a state imposes these kinds of restrictions on women just in order to make it more expensive for them to get an abortion, then what it does is just as wrong as what it does when it makes it illegal for women to be offered abortion coverage as part of their comprehensive health insurance policies. We can see this by going back to the cases where Alice and Shimp don't have much money and by asking what we'd say about the state doing this kind of thing to Shimp in such a case. So suppose Shimp tells the doctor he wants to be disconnected from the bone marrow transferring machine right away and the doctor tells him how much it will cost him to be disconnected. When Shimp looks at the bill, he sees the total comes out to $1,000 more than he can afford. The doctor then says, "Sorry, I'd be happy to charge you $1,000 less than this, but we have to follow these rules the state came up with because they wanted to make it cost $1,000 more." The same kind of reason for thinking it would be wrong for the state to prevent Shimp from being offered a comprehensive health insurance policy that would cover the cost of his being disconnected from the machine is also a reason to think it would be wrong for the state to try to increase the costs of being disconnected from the machine by forcing him to pay for additional expenses.

First, if Shimp had enough money to cover the total costs of being disconnected from the bone marrow transferring machine, it would be wrong for the state to steal $1,000 from him so that he no longer had enough money to cover the costs. Second, if it would be wrong for the state to steal $1,000 from Shimp so he no longer had enough money to cover the costs, it would be wrong for the state to raise the cost of being disconnected by $1,000 so he no longer had enough money to cover the costs. Either it's okay for the state to try to prevent Shimp from being able to afford to be disconnected from the machine or it isn't. So if it would be wrong for the state to steal money from Shimp so he couldn't afford to be disconnected from the machine, it would also be wrong for the state to raise the cost of being disconnected from the machine so he no longer had enough money to afford to be disconnected.

And if that's what we should say about this version of the story of McFall and Shimp, that's what we should also say about this version of the case of Al and Alice. It would be wrong for the state to steal money from Alice to prevent her from being able to afford an abortion, and if it would be wrong for the state to do this, it would be wrong for the state to raise the cost of her getting an abortion to prevent her from being able to afford an abortion. In the case of laws that prevent women from being offered abortion coverage as part of their comprehensive health insurance policies, this kind of reasoning also applied to cases where Alice wasn't poor and to cases where the abortion was sought by Barbara, Carol, Dorothy, Elaine, or any other woman seeking a legal abortion. So the same kind of reasoning would apply here, too. If a state imposes restrictions on abortion as a way of trying to prevent women from being able to afford to get one, it does something wrong. That's what you should think if you think it would be wrong for the state to do this kind of thing to Shimp. And since that's what you should think about the case of McFall and Shimp even though McFall was a person with a right to life, that's what you should think about these kinds of abortion restrictions even if you think every fetus is a person with a right to life.

Of course, a defender of such restrictions might deny that the point of the restrictions is to make abortions more expensive. They might say the point of the restrictions is simply to ensure that women have the time and information they need to make an informed and considered decision about whether they really want to have an abortion in the first place. There's a simple way to test this claim. We can ask the defender of these restrictions whether they would continue to favor them even if the restrictions didn't make abortions more difficult to obtain. Take the case of mandatory ultrasounds. If the point of requiring a woman to have an ultrasound before she can have an abortion is to make it more expensive for her to have an abortion, then the requirement would lose its point if the state covered the costs of the ultrasound. But if the point of the requirement is to help her make an informed and considered decision, there's no reason to insist that she pay for the ultrasound herself rather than having the state pay for it. The same goes for mandatory abortion counseling and for the mandatory waiting period itself. If the point of requiring the counseling to take place in person rather than by phone is to make abortions more expensive by forcing women who want abortions to make two trips to the clinic rather than one, then women who want abortions should be forced to pay the extra costs involved themselves. If the point is simply to make sure women considering abortion receive adequate information, there's no reason to bill them for the extra expenses. If the point of the waiting period is to force women who want abortions to spend more money on things like gas, child care, and hotel rooms, then they should be forced to cover those costs, too. But if the point is simply to make sure they have enough time to make a thoughtful decision, there's no reason for the state not to cover these costs for them as well.

If a defender of mandatory waiting periods, abortion counseling, or ultrasounds admits the requirements they favor would lose their point if the women in question didn't have to pay for them, then I've already told you why I think you should find their position objectionable. You should find their position objectionable for the same reason you should find it objectionable to prevent women from being offered abortion coverage as part of their comprehensive health insurance policies. But some defenders of these kinds of requirements might be willing to agree that the requirements shouldn't be used as a device for imposing financial hardships on women who want abortions. They might say, for example, that the requirement that a woman have an ultrasound before she has an abortion is justified even if she doesn't have to pay for it. So let's assume, at least for the sake of the argument, that the state is willing to compensate women for the expenses it imposes on them when it imposes mandatory waiting periods, abortion counseling, or ultrasounds. If the state were willing to compensate them for these expenses, would it still be wrong for it to impose these kinds of requirements? Let's take them one at a time.

I'll start with the waiting period itself. So forget about counseling and ultrasounds for a moment and suppose a state's law simply says when a woman contacts a clinic to request an abortion, the clinic has to wait a certain amount of time before it's allowed to give her one. Let's say the length of the waiting period is about average for states that have waiting periods and call it 48 hours. And let's suppose this state is willing to compensate women for any additional expenses the wait might impose on them. So all this particular law would do is force these women to wait. Suppose, to keep things simple, that Alice happens to live next door to an abortion clinic. The moment she finds out she's pregnant, she rushes into the waiting room and says she wants an abortion right away. It turns out a patient just cancelled and a doctor is available at this very moment. And the doctor says as far as he's concerned, he'd be happy to perform the procedure as soon as Alice gives her informed consent to it. But, he explains, the law won't let her have an abortion right now. She'll have to come back in 48 hours. Would it be okay for the state to make Alice wait in this way?

Let's see if our friends McFall and Shimp can help us out again. This time, we'll need a version of their story where Shimp says he wants to be unplugged from the bone marrow transferring machine right away and the doctor says he can't do that because the law says he has to wait 48 hours first. As I was originally picturing the story, 48 hours would be more than enough time for McFall to get the bone marrow he needs. So we'll have to make another change to the story. Let's say the bone marrow transferring machine works very slowly and Shimp would have to stay connected to it for a few weeks in order to save McFall's life. Shimp wakes up in the hospital, and as soon as the situation is explained to him, he says he wants to be disconnected right away. The doctor then says he'd be happy to do that but he can't because the state has a mandatory waiting period. But don't worry, he adds, we can disconnect you in a couple of days. This version of the story makes Shimp's waiting period more like Alice's. Do you think it would be okay for the state to make Shimp wait in this way?

One reason the state's treatment of Shimp might strike you as wrong here is this: it's patronizing. Shimp is a grown man but this kind of law treats him like a little boy. "Are you really sure you want to do that? Why don't you take some time to think about it first." That sounds like the kind of thing a parent might say to a young child, not the kind of thing we'd expect a well-ordered state to say to one of its adult citizens. Try to put yourself in Shimp's situation here. Would you feel insulted by the way the state was treating you? Demeaned? Disrespected? I'm guessing you would. If that's right, you should think it would be reasonable for Alice to feel the same way when the state forces her to wait 48 hours before she can get an abortion. And that might seem like a good reason to think mandatory waiting periods for women who want abortions are wrong.

You might find this a good reason to think abortion waiting periods are wrong, but I'm not sure you'll think it's a good enough reason. That's because there are other cases where states impose waiting periods on people before they're allowed to do things they want to do, and in these other cases, many people seem to think it's fine for the states to do that. If you think it's okay for states to impose waiting periods in these other cases, and if imposing waiting periods in these other cases also seems patronizing, then you can't say the fact that abortion waiting periods seem patronizing is a good enough reason to think abortion waiting periods are wrong.

Many states, for example, make you wait to get a marriage license. South Carolina makes you wait a day from the time you apply for the license to the time you receive it and Maryland makes you wait two days, but most states with this kind of requirement make you wait three days. Some make you wait even longer. A handful of other states make you wait a day or more from the time you receive your marriage license to the time you can use it. Some states have both kinds of waiting period. In New Hampshire, you have to wait three days to get your license after you apply for it and wait another three days to use your license after you get it. In one way or another, the majority of states in this country make it illegal for you to get married on the day you decide to get married.

The same goes for deciding you don't want to be married anymore. Many states impose a mandatory separation or waiting period for couples who want to get a no-fault divorce. If you and your spouse decide to get divorced in Alabama, for example, the state will make you wait a month. Iowa and Washington will make you wait three months. Every other state with a waiting period will make you wait even longer: six months, a year, eighteen months in the case of Arkansas. And if you have a child at some point along the way and want to give the child up for adoption, plenty of states will make you wait to do that, too. In a number of states, to take a typical example, a woman who gives birth has to wait 72 hours before she can sign the relevant consent form.

As far as I can tell, there's only one reason for these kinds of laws. Getting married, getting divorced, giving up a kid for adoption—these are big decisions that have serious consequences. People sometimes make them impulsively and live to regret their mistakes. So the state makes sure they take a bit of time to think things over before they act. Sometimes more than just a bit of time. Again, as far as I can tell, plenty of people seem to think it's fine for the state to do this. You may well be one of them. And if you are, you can't object to abortion waiting periods by saying they're patronizing. After all, these other waiting periods seem patronizing, too.

This doesn't mean you shouldn't object to abortion waiting periods. I think you should object to them. But unless you object to all mandatory waiting periods as a matter of principle, you should object to abortion waiting periods for a different kind of reason. To do that, you'll need a reason that explains why it would be wrong for the state to make Shimp wait 48 hours before being disconnected from the bone marrow transferring machine. You'll have to make sure this reason also applies to the case where the state makes Alice wait 48 hours before she can have an abortion. But you'll also have to make sure the reason doesn't apply to cases where the state imposes waiting periods for getting married or divorced or for giving up a child for adoption. If you find a reason that meets these requirements, then you'll have a good reason to object to mandatory abortion waiting periods that won't commit you to opposing mandatory marriage, divorce, or adoption waiting periods. And I think there's a good reason that fits the bill.

What I have in mind is this. When the state forces Shimp to wait 48 hours before being disconnected from the bone marrow transferring machine, it forces him to spend 48 hours letting someone use his body who has no right to use it. It's wrong for the state to force a person to spend 48 hours letting someone use their body who has no right to use it. This is enough to make it wrong for the state to impose such a waiting period on Shimp. If the state forces Alice to wait 48 hours before having an abortion, it forces Alice to spend 48 hours letting someone use her body who has no right to use it. So this second reason to think it's wrong to force Shimp to wait is also a reason to think it's wrong to force Alice to wait. But if the state makes someone wait 48 hours before they can get married or divorced or before they can give their child up for adoption, it doesn't force them to spend 48 hours letting someone do something with their body that they have no right to do. So this second reason for thinking it's wrong to force Shimp and Alice to wait doesn't mean you should also think it's wrong to force people to wait before getting married or divorced or before giving their child up for adoption.

This second objection to mandatory abortion waiting periods depends on several claims. Let me go back through them in order and see if I can convince you that each of them is true. The first claim is that if the state forces Shimp to wait 48 hours before being disconnected from the bone marrow transferring machine, it forces him to spend 48 hours letting someone use his body who has no right to use it. This claim seems hard to deny. If I prevent you from ending a situation, I force you to continue it. If I prevent you from leaving a party, for example, I force you to stay. These are just two sides of the same coin. And if you agree with the judge's decision in *McFall v. Shimp*, you agree that McFall had no right to use Shimp's body. So preventing Shimp from ending the situation where McFall is using his body for 48 hours means forcing Shimp to let someone use his body who has no right to use it for 48 hours.

The second claim is that it's wrong for the state to force a person to spend 48 hours letting someone use their body who has no right to use it. If you agree with the judge's decision in the actual case of *McFall v. Shimp*, you'll have to agree with this claim, too. After all, in the actual case of *McFall v. Shimp*, it would have taken Shimp less than 48 hours to donate the bone marrow McFall needed. If you agreed with the judge's decision in that case, then you agree it would be wrong for the state to force a person to let someone use their body who has no right to use it even if doing so would take less than 48 hours. And if you agree it would be wrong for the state to do this when it would take less than 48 hours to do it, you'll surely agree it would be wrong for the state to do this if it would take 48 hours to do it. So you should agree that if the state forces Shimp to wait 48 hours before being disconnected from the bone marrow transferring machine, it forces him to spend 48 hours letting someone use his body who has no right to use it, and you should agree that it would be wrong for the state to force Shimp to spend 48 hours letting someone use his body who has no right to use it. And as long as you agree with those two claims, you should agree that it would be wrong for the state to force Shimp to wait 48 hours before being disconnected from the bone marrow transferring machine.

The third claim is that if the state forces Alice to wait 48 hours before having an abortion, it forces her to spend 48 hours letting someone use her body who has no right to use it. Again, preventing someone from ending a situation means forcing them to continue enduring it. If you can't leave the party, you have to stay. So making Alice wait 48 hours before she can have an abortion means forcing Alice to let Al use her body for 48 hours. And since I'm assuming at this point that my argument in part I has been successful, I'm assuming at least for the sake of the argument here that you agree that Al doesn't have the right to use Alice's body. So preventing Alice from ending the situation where Al is using her body means forcing Alice to let someone use her body who has no right to use it. And if forcing someone to do this is enough to make it wrong for the state to force Shimp to wait 48 hours before being disconnected from the bone marrow transferring machine, then it's also enough to make it wrong for the state to force Alice to wait 48 hours before having an abortion.

The fourth and final claim is that endorsing this reason for opposing mandatory abortion waiting periods doesn't commit you to opposing mandatory waiting periods in the case of marriage, divorce, or adoption. Let's take those cases one at a time. Suppose you and your beloved got engaged just moments ago and the two of you want to get married right away. The state says you have to wait a few days. When the state forces you to wait 48 hours before you can get married, it doesn't force you to spend 48 hours letting someone else use your body in a way they have no right to use it. Not being married to someone doesn't give them the right to use your body in a way you don't want them to use it. Suppose a few years later the two of you decide to call it quits and you want the divorce to become effective immediately. Again, the state says you have to wait. This doesn't force you to let someone else use your body in a way they have no right to use it, either. Not yet being divorced from someone doesn't give them the right to use your body in a way you don't want them to use it. And the same goes for the woman who just gave birth and is already sure she wants to give her child up for adoption. If the state makes her wait a few days before she can permanently sign away her parental rights, this doesn't force her to let anyone use her body in a way they have no right to use it. She's perfectly free to have someone else take care of the child from the moment it's born, for example. She simply can't give away her parental rights on a permanent basis until she takes a few days to think it over and make sure that's her final decision.

If you find the whole idea of legally imposed waiting periods objectionably patronizing, you'll have two good reasons to oppose mandatory waiting periods for abortion. But even if you're okay with the state imposing waiting periods on people who want to get married or divorced or who want to give their child up for adoption, you'll still have one good reason to oppose waiting periods for abortion. And since the reason you'll have is based your reaction to the case of McFall and Shimp, and since McFall was clearly a person with a right to life, you'll have a good reason to oppose mandatory waiting periods for abortion even if you think every fetus is a person with a right to life.

# 25

## Mandatory Counseling

Every state that makes women wait before they can have an abortion also makes women receive counseling before they can have an abortion. They have to get the counseling first, and once they get it, the waiting period begins. But not every state that makes women receive counseling before they can have an abortion also forces them to wait after they've gotten the counseling. In these states, a woman is allowed to get an abortion as soon as she's able to schedule an appointment, as long as the appointment includes some form of abortion counseling. What particular form the counseling has to take varies from state to state. But what's true in every state is this: the state could decide to require abortion counseling without also requiring a waiting period. So just because it's wrong for a state to require women to wait before they get an abortion, that doesn't mean it's also wrong for a state to require women to receive abortion counseling before they get an abortion. Whether mandatory abortion counseling itself is wrong is a separate question. What should we say about it?

Let's see what McFall and Shimp might have to teach us here. Suppose Shimp wakes up in the hospital, and as soon as he realizes what's going on, he demands to be disconnected from the bone marrow transferring machine and says he's ready to read and sign the consent form. The doctor immediately rushes over to Shimp and says he'll be happy to disconnect him from the machine as soon as Shimp reads and signs the form, but first he has to take care of one thing that's required as a matter of state law. And let's suppose, just to get things started, that the one thing the doctor has to do is this: he has to offer to let Shimp see a pamphlet with additional information if Shimp wants to look at it. Simply making the doctor offer to let Shimp see a pamphlet if Shimp wants to see it is a pretty modest requirement. So you might be inclined to think at least this much would be okay. But I haven't said anything about what information the pamphlet contains yet. So let's wait a bit before we pass judgment.

Suppose there are rumors floating around on the internet that say disconnecting Shimp from the bone marrow transferring machine before McFall gets enough bone marrow would increase Shimp's risk of getting cancer. And suppose the cancer research community says there's no credible evidence to support this claim. Would it be okay for the pamphlet to try to scare Shimp into staying connected to the machine by telling him he'll probably get cancer if he's disconnected from it now? I assume you'll agree this would be wrong. Even if the doctor doesn't have to force Shimp to read the pamphlet, it would be wrong simply to make the doctor offer the pamphlet to Shimp if it contained unsupported claims of this sort. And this is true even though McFall is a person with a right to life. Assuming you agree with this claim in the case of Shimp, you should say the same about the case of Alice. If the pamphlet says abortions cause breast cancer and if the cancer research community says there's no credible evidence to support this claim, for example, you should agree that it would be wrong to offer Alice a pamphlet telling her she'll probably get cancer if she has an abortion. And if it would be wrong to offer Alice a pamphlet like that, it would be wrong for the state to force Alice's doctor to offer her a pamphlet like that before she's allowed to have an abortion.

Now suppose all the information in the pamphlet is accurate. It turns out there really are some risks to Shimp associated with disconnecting him from the machine right now, and the pamphlet explains these risks in clear and accessible terms. It correctly describes each of the physical problems some people have experienced after being prematurely disconnected from bone marrow transferring machines, and it accurately reports the number of times each problem has occurred compared to the number of times it hasn't. And it does the same for any emotional or psychological problems that people may have experienced after being prematurely disconnected from bone marrow transferring machines. If the pamphlet is completely clear and accurate in all these respects and if every word in the pamphlet is true, this might seem enough to make it okay to force the doctor to offer it to Shimp before he is allowed to have Shimp read and sign the consent form and then disconnect Shimp from the machine. But even this, I think, isn't enough to make it okay.

Here's why. Suppose there are also some risks to Shimp if he stays connected to the machine. And suppose the pamphlet deliberately conceals these risks from Shimp. Even if everything the pamphlet says about the risks to Shimp of being disconnected from the machine right now is clear, accurate, and thorough, it would still be wrong to offer Shimp the pamphlet unless it told an equally clear and accurate story about the risks to Shimp of not being disconnected from the machine right now. I'm pretty sure you'll agree with this claim because I'm pretty sure you'd feel entitled to be told both sides of the story if your doctor gave you information about a procedure you were thinking of having done. And if you do agree with this claim, you'll have to say the same thing about Alice. It wouldn't be enough to make sure the pamphlet was accurate about the physical and psychological risks to Alice of having an abortion. It would also have to be equally comprehensive and accurate about the physical and psychological risks to Alice of carrying an unwanted pregnancy to term. If the pamphlet correctly notes there is a remote risk that a woman can die from having an abortion, for example, it would have to also note that there is a considerably greater risk that she will die from childbirth. If the pamphlet was clear and accurate and balanced in all these respects, though, then I, at least, can't see what would be wrong with offering it to Alice. I'll go ahead and assume you can't see anything wrong with it, either.

Of course, there's a difference between saying it would be okay for a doctor to offer Alice a balanced and accurate pamphlet with additional information before she reads and signs the consent form and saying it's okay for the state to prevent Alice from having an abortion until the doctor offers her one. If you're sufficiently worked up about the evils of the nanny state, you might find even this restriction on Alice's freedom objectionable. If Alice wants more information before she reads and signs the consent form, you might say, let her ask for it. If she doesn't, let her go ahead and read and sign the consent form now and get her abortion over with without the doctor's having to waste her time offering her additional information she isn't interested in. But I'm going to assume, at least for the sake of the argument, that you don't think there's anything wrong with saying Shimp and Alice each have to be offered access to this kind of additional information before they're allowed to read and sign the consent forms for the procedures they've requested. And if that's the case, you should agree that mandatory abortion counseling can be okay if it's not combined with a mandatory waiting period, at least in principle, even if the way many states currently carry it out might turn out to be inaccurate and unbalanced, and so not okay in practice.

I've focused so far on the least intrusive kind of mandatory abortion counseling—the kind where the doctor simply has to offer the woman a pamphlet containing additional information but the woman doesn't have to take it. Over half the states in this country require abortion counseling before a woman can have an abortion, and over half of these states treat the written information involved as something that simply has to be offered to her. But that still leaves a number of states that require more than this, including some states with pretty big populations like Ohio, Michigan, and Missouri. In these states, doctors aren't simply required to *offer* to give the additional written information. They're required to actually *give* it to the woman before they are allowed to perform an abortion. This means a lot of women in this country don't have the right to say no to the offer if they want to have an abortion. They have to let the doctor give them the pamphlet first. Are laws that impose this kind of mandatory counseling wrong?

The answer might be less clear in this case. On the one hand, forcing a woman to take a pamphlet isn't the same as forcing her to read it. She's just as free not to look at it in this case as she is in the case where the doctor offers to give it to her and she says no thank you. On the other hand, it's hard to see why the state would make the doctor give it to her and not simply make the doctor offer to give it to her unless the idea is that once it's right there in her hands she'll find it hard to resist looking at it. In that sense, this form of mandatory abortion counseling seems manipulative in a way that just saying the doctor has to offer to give her a pamphlet containing some additional information isn't. But is it objectionably manipulative? That depends on what you'd say about a parallel case involving Shimp.

If Shimp says he doesn't want to look at the pamphlet and the doctor says the law still requires him to give the pamphlet to him before he can let Shimp read and sign the consent form and be disconnected from the machine, would you find that law objectionable? I don't really know what to expect here. There's not much of a consensus in this country about whether it's okay for the state to try to manipulate people in this kind of way. Some people think this kind of calculated nudging by the state is perfectly fine and that it fully respects the freedom and autonomy of its citizens. Others find it disturbing. So I'll just say if you think it would be okay for the state to do this in the case of Shimp, then you should think it would be okay for the state to do it in the case of Alice, and if you don't, then you shouldn't.

I've focused so far on the written form of mandatory abortion counseling. What about the verbal kind? Most states that require abortion counseling before a woman can consent to an abortion, for example, require the doctor to provide a description of the specific procedure the woman is consenting to. And virtually all the states that do this require the doctor to provide the information verbally rather than in writing. If the description the doctor provides is sufficiently clear, accurate, and balanced, I'll assume you wouldn't object if the law required the doctor to provide it in the form of a pamphlet. Assuming that's right, is there any reason you should object if the law requires the doctor to present it verbally instead?

There might be. To figure this out, let's go back to the case of Shimp again and start with the version of the story where all the doctor has to do is offer Shimp a pamphlet containing the extra information. I said I wasn't sure you'd think it makes a difference if instead of simply offering Shimp the pamphlet, the law said the doctor had to actually give the pamphlet to him. And part of the reason I wasn't sure you'd think this made a difference is that either way, Shimp would be free not to read it if he didn't want to. Forcing Shimp to actually take the pamphlet rather than simply having it offered to him might seem a bit manipulative, maybe even objectionably manipulative, but it also might seem like it's just not that big a deal.

But now suppose the law said the doctor doesn't just have to give the pamphlet to Shimp. It says he actually has to force

Shimp to read it. At this point, I wouldn't be surprised if you said enough is enough. It's one thing to make sure Shimp has access to this additional information before he reads and signs the consent form, maybe even to tempt him into looking at it by putting it in his hands before he reads and signs the form, but it may well seem like another thing altogether to force him to read it. Shimp's a grown man. Maybe you're okay with the state making sure he has access to this extra information even if he didn't ask for it, but even if you are, you may well draw the line at forcing him to read it if he doesn't want to.

Let's suppose that's your reaction. If it is, you should consider the fact that forcing Shimp to read the pamphlet doesn't seem very different from forcing him to sit there while the doctor reads it to him. I suppose he could cover his ears and yell "I'm not listening! I'm not listening!" But practically speaking, having to sit there while the doctor reads the pamphlet to him makes it just as impossible for him to avoid getting the additional information as being forced to read it does. So if you think it would be wrong for the state to force Shimp to read the pamphlet containing the extra information, you should think it would be wrong for the state to insist the doctor has to read it to him. If you think that, you should think it would be wrong for the state to say he can't be unplugged from the machine until the doctor gives him the information verbally. And if you think that, you should think it would be wrong for the state to say Alice can't have her abortion until the doctor gives her the extra information verbally, too. Even if the content of the information in question is unobjectionable, you should insist that if the state's going to make it part of a requirement for having an abortion, the requirement should be limited to providing the additional information in written form.

I've focused so far on information about Alice: what the procedure will do to her and what effects the procedure might have on her. But what about Al? Virtually every state that requires a woman to receive counseling before she's allowed to give her consent to having an abortion includes telling her the gestational age of the fetus she's carrying as one of its requirements. Most also require her to be offered or given written information about fetal development through all stages of pregnancy. And about a third of the states that require abortion counseling say the woman has to be offered or given information about whether the fetus is able to feel pain, though a few of these states require this only in those rare cases where the woman is already well into her second trimester. I'll again assume you agree it would be wrong for the state to do this if the information the woman is offered or given is false or deceptively unbalanced. But let's assume the information about the fetus is clear, accurate, and fairly presented. Is there anything wrong with requiring a woman to be offered or given it before she's allowed to have an abortion?

This might at first seem to be the biggest problem with mandatory abortion counseling laws. If you go to a doctor to get your appendix or cataracts removed, you expect the doctor to tell you what the procedure will do to you and what its likely side effects on you will be, but you'd probably be taken aback if they said they couldn't do the procedure until they also told you about the effects it might have on other people. In fact, in the case of every medical procedure you might be able to think of other than abortion, you might think it's fine for the state to require the patient to be offered or given information about the procedure's expected effects on the patient, but not so fine for it to require the patient to be offered or given information about its expected effects on other people. And if that's what you think, you might be inclined to find this element of mandatory abortion counseling laws objectionable. If you should be able to get other procedures done without being lectured about their effects on other people, you might be inclined to think that Alice should be able to get her abortion without being lectured about the effects this would have on Al, too, even if Al is a person with a right to life.

This inclination is understandable. But I'm not so sure you should give in to it. Once again, the story of McFall and Shimp can help us figure this out. Suppose Shimp wakes up in the hospital and as soon as he realizes what's going on, he demands to be given a consent form to sign so he can be disconnected from the bone marrow transferring machine. The doctor says he'd be more than happy to take care of that, but he's required by law to tell Shimp two things before he can get Shimp's consent to proceed. First, he has to tell Shimp how much longer it would take for McFall to get all the bone marrow he needs. Second, he has to tell Shimp whether McFall is currently in a coma and, if he isn't, whether the process of disconnecting Shimp from the machine will cause McFall any pain. Once he tells Shimp these two things, he'll go ahead and disconnect Shimp from the machine if Shimp still wants to sign the consent form. But the law says he can't do that if he hasn't told Shimp these two things first.

These two requirements may not strike you as particularly unreasonable in this case. First of all, Shimp might be confused about how much bone marrow McFall needs or about how quickly the bone marrow transferring machine works. He might be under the impression that he'd have to stay hooked up to the machine for the next few months in order to save McFall's life when in fact he'd only have to stay hooked up to it for a few more hours. Now maybe getting clear about the facts of the case wouldn't make a difference to Shimp. But maybe it would. If his decision was only going to affect his own well-being, it might seem a bit too nanny state to insist that he be given the information if he doesn't want to hear about it. But he isn't just making a decision about his own body. He's making a life or death decision about McFall's. Given that McFall's life stands in the balance and that it's at least possible Shimp would change his mind if he knew how close McFall was to getting all the bone marrow he needs, you may well think it's fine if the doctor says he can't disconnect Shimp from the machine without telling him this first. You might even think it would be positively irresponsible for the doctor to disconnect Shimp from the machine without telling him this first. In that case, you'd think not just that it's okay for a state to have this requirement but that it would be wrong for a state not to have it.

The same sort of thing seems true in the case of the second requirement. Shimp might have heard that McFall is in a coma but he might not understand what this means. He might be making an assumption about whether McFall is conscious or about whether McFall will feel any pain if he's disconnected from the machine. Now maybe Shimp isn't making any assumptions about this. And maybe even if he is, they wouldn't make a difference to his decision. But, again, maybe he is and maybe they would. Since McFall's life is in Shimp's hands and since it's at least possible that these facts would have an impact on Shimp's decision, it again strikes me as plausible that you won't object if the doctor isn't allowed to disconnect Shimp from the machine without first setting Shimp straight about these facts. Again, you might even think it would be wrong for the doctor not to do so first.

Regardless of whether you think it would be wrong not to require the doctor to tell Shimp these two things before Shimp can consent to being disconnected from the machine, let's suppose you at least think it would be okay if the state did require the doctor to do this. If that's right, then you should think the same thing about two parallel requirements in the case of Alice. First, Alice might be mistaken about how far along her pregnancy is. She was unconscious when she was raped and only figured out that it had happened at all when she found out she was pregnant. She's been assuming it happened about a month ago, but maybe she's already five months pregnant. She might have to spend much less time carrying her pregnancy to term at this point than she thinks. This difference might not make a difference to Alice, but then again it might. And Al's life hangs in the balance. If you think that was enough to make it okay to say Shimp can't consent to being disconnected from the machine until he knows how much longer he'd have to stay connected to it to keep McFall alive, then you should think it's enough to make it okay to say Alice can't consent to having an abortion until she knows how much longer she'd have to stay pregnant to keep Al alive.

And the same goes for the second requirement. Alice might be making an assumption about whether Al's conscious at this stage in his fetal development or about whether he'll feel any pain if she has an abortion. She might not be making any assumptions about this, of course, and even if she is, they might not make any difference to her decision. But Al's life hangs in the balance and knowing the facts might make a difference. If you think that's enough to make it okay to say Shimp can't consent to being disconnected from the machine until he knows whether McFall is conscious or will feel pain from the disconnection, then you should think it's enough to make it okay to say Alice can't consent to having an abortion until she's told whatever the doctors can tell her about whether Al is conscious or will feel pain from her having an abortion.

It may well be objectionable for the state to make Alice get more information about the effect the abortion will have on her than just what she would need to know to read and sign the consent form. But even if it is, that doesn't mean it would be wrong for the state to make sure she understands some basic facts about Al before she consents to having an abortion. Either way, many forms of mandatory counseling that are currently imposed on women who seek abortions turn out to be unjustified. But that doesn't have to mean that all forms of mandatory counseling are.

# 26

## Mandatory Ultrasounds

GoFundMe is a popular crowdfunding website. It helps people raise money for a variety of purposes. The most common categories tend to involve helping people when something bad has happened: funeral expenses for a loved one, costs of rebuilding after a fire, medical bills for a pet or family member. The way it works is you set up a personalized campaign webpage and ask people to share it via social media. They can make donations in any amount directly through the page itself and they can pass the link along to their friends and family. If you want to start your own fundraising campaign on GoFundMe, the first thing you do is give your campaign a title and set a fundraising goal. After you enter that information along with your Zip code, you're led to a page that directs you to add a photo. That page contains these words: "Great photos will help your campaign raise more money. A photo is required."

Why does GoFundMe make you use a photo on your fundraising page? The answer is simple. They keep a few pennies from each dollar that's donated, so the more you raise, the more they make. And they know from experience—over three billion dollars' worth of experience—that pictures are effective. Why are they effective? It's not because they add information. The pictures on GoFundMe pages don't tell you anything you can't learn from the text that goes along with them. If the picture shows a soldier or firefighter in uniform, you can bet the page that goes along with it tells you they're a soldier or a firefighter. If the page says a mother of five is struggling to pay her medical bills, you can be sure all five kids will be smiling for the camera alongside her. So the pictures don't give you further information. What they do is tug at your heartstrings. They arouse your feelings of sympathy and compassion. If you get an email saying the young daughter of a friend of a friend has leukemia and the family is asking for donations to help pay the bills, it's not that hard to click "delete" and get on with your day. If a striking picture of the adorable little girl pops up on your Facebook feed, though, it's quite a bit harder to say no.

I mention this here because this seems to be the idea behind laws requiring women to get an ultrasound before they can have an abortion. Typically there's no medical reason for a doctor to do an ultrasound before performing an abortion, and if there's no medical reason for doing one, it's hard to think of any other reason for requiring that one be done if the point isn't to make it psychologically harder for the woman to go through with her decision to have the abortion. As was the case with mandatory abortion counseling, laws requiring an ultrasound are often tied up with laws requiring a waiting period. In Arizona, Louisiana, and Virginia, for example, a woman has to wait 24 hours after having an ultrasound before she's allowed to have an abortion. But, as was also the case with mandatory abortion counseling, ultrasounds can be pried apart from mandatory waiting periods in principle even if they generally go hand in hand in practice. So suppose a state decides to have an ultrasound requirement but doesn't impose a waiting period after the ultrasound has been performed. Would that requirement by itself be okay?

Let's see what we'd think about a similar requirement in the case of McFall and Shimp. So suppose Shimp had never met his cousin and McFall was stuck in the hospital, too sick to attend the hearing. The judge rules in Shimp's favor, but before he concludes the hearing McFall's lawyer makes the following request: "Your Honor, if you're not going force Mr. Shimp to give my client the bone marrow he needs, I respectfully ask you to at least force him to go down to the hospital and look Mr. McFall in the eye and tell him he's not going to help him out." The judge responds by saying he will do no such thing. And he will do no such thing because the state simply has no right to make Shimp do this. I take it you'd agree with the judge on this point. Now suppose McFall's lawyer then says, "Will you at least force Mr. Shimp to look at a picture of my client?" Again, the judge says no. Mr. Shimp has the right not to look at a picture of Mr. McFall if he doesn't want to. I again suspect you'll agree with the judge here. "Well, how about this," McFall's lawyer responds, "we take a picture of Mr. McFall and hold it in front of his face, but we let him look away from it if he wants to. Will you at least force Mr. Shimp to put up with this much before letting him refuse to give my client the bone marrow he needs?" At this point, the judge becomes exasperated with McFall's lawyer. You're probably exasperated at this point, too. Do you think it would be okay for the state to say Shimp has to let someone put a picture of McFall in front of his face if he wants to avoid being forced to let McFall have his bone marrow? Probably not.

But now consider this: if Alice lives in Louisiana, Texas, or Wisconsin and wants to get an abortion there, the law says not only that she has to have an ultrasound first but also that the abortion provider has to display the image and describe it to her. Strictly speaking, the laws in these states don't literally force Alice to look at the image. She retains her right to look away from it if she wants to. Still, if you agree it would be wrong for the state to force Shimp to put up with this kind of thing in order for him to avoid being forced to let McFall use his bone marrow, you should agree it's wrong for these states to force Alice to put up with this in order for her to avoid being forced to let Al use her uterus. And since you think it would be wrong for the state to exert this kind of psychological pressure on Shimp even though McFall is a person with a right to life, you should think it's wrong for these states to do this to Alice even if you think Al, too, is a person with a right to life. Even if no waiting period is attached to the requirement, even if the state offers to pay for the costs of the ultrasound, and even if the woman is not literally forced to look at the image itself, laws that say she can't have an abortion until she has a medically unnecessary ultrasound and is shown the resulting image are morally unacceptable. And they're morally unacceptable even if every fetus is a person with a right to life.

Laws requiring a pregnant woman to have an ultrasound and to be shown the results before she can have an abortion represent the strongest form of ultrasound requirement currently on the books. A number of other states have a more modest requirement. In states like Ohio, Indiana, North Carolina, and Florida, Alice would still have to have an ultrasound performed before she could get an abortion, but the abortion provider wouldn't be required to show her the image. The provider would simply be required to offer to show her the image if she wanted to see it. What should we make of this more modest kind of requirement?

That, too, depends on what we'd say about a similar case involving McFall and Shimp. Suppose, just to get things started, McFall's lawyer makes the following proposal: "Mr. Shimp is not allowed to say no to giving Mr. McFall his bone marrow until we take a picture of Mr. McFall and offer to show it to Mr. Shimp. Mr. Shimp doesn't have to accept the offer to look at the picture, but he does have to give Mr. McFall the bone marrow if he refuses to at least be offered a chance to look at a picture of Mr. McFall." That's a relatively modest proposal but I still get the sense the judge would dismiss it out of hand. McFall simply has no right to Shimp's bone marrow, so Shimp has the right not to give it to him. That's the crux of the case. And since Shimp has the right not to give McFall the bone marrow, he has the right not to give McFall the bone marrow even if he hasn't been offered a chance to look at a picture of McFall. I have a feeling you'll think that, too. If that's right, you should say the same thing about Alice. Not only is it wrong for a state to say she has to be shown an ultrasound before she can have an abortion but it's also wrong for a state to say she has to be offered the chance to view an ultrasound before she can have an abortion.

I think you'll probably agree it would be wrong for a state to require even this much of Shimp. But even if you don't agree, there's another reason you should think it would be wrong for the state to require this much of Alice. That's because the mere act of taking a picture of McFall imposes no burden on Shimp, but the act of generating an ultrasound image of Al does impose a burden on Alice. And if we revise the story of McFall and Shimp to take this difference into account, I'm pretty sure the result will be a story where you'll agree it would be wrong for the state to require even this much of Shimp.

The vast majority of abortions take place during the first trimester, and in most of these cases, a doctor would have to insert a probe into the woman's vagina in order to produce a satisfactory image. Shimp, of course, didn't have a vagina, but suppose for a moment that David Shimp had actually been Diana Shimp and that for some reason the only way they could take a picture of McFall involved inserting a probe into Shimp's vagina. Even if you were assured that insertion of the probe was completely painless, I'm pretty sure you'd think it would be wrong for the state to say Shimp has to give McFall the bone marrow unless Shimp first allows the probe to be inserted in her vagina so the picture of McFall can be taken. Assuming that's right, you should think it would be wrong for the state to say Alice has to have a medically unnecessary ultrasound done in this way before she can have an abortion even if no one has to show Alice the resulting image after it's been done.

If Alice's pregnancy is further along, a considerably less invasive form of ultrasound becomes possible. This is what most people have in mind when they think of an ultrasound. Alice just has to lie back on an examination table while someone coats her abdomen with a layer of gel and then lie there some more while the doctor glides a device over her belly. This may not sound like such a big deal. Still, I bet you'll agree it would be wrong for the state to say Shimp has to give McFall his bone marrow unless he first helps them take a picture of McFall if taking a picture of McFall would require Shimp to undergo the same kind of treatment. Assuming that's so, you should agree it's wrong for the state to say Alice has to let Al use her uterus unless she first has an ultrasound done regardless of whether the ultrasound is transvaginal or the more familiar kind. And assuming you agree this would be wrong in the case of Shimp and McFall even though McFall is a person with a right to life, you should agree this is so of Alice and Al even if you think Al is a person with a right to life. A picture may be worth a thousand words, but even if it turns out to be okay for the state to say Alice has to be offered a pamphlet containing a thousand words before she can have an abortion, it's not okay to say she has to be offered a picture if taking the picture requires her to be treated in these ways.

# 27

## Parental Consent and Notification

Jane turned 17 a few weeks ago and found out she was pregnant a few days later. She's only been with one guy so far, so she knows who the father is. And he's been pretty good about it, telling her he'll support whatever decision she makes. She's expecting a boy and has already decided she'd want to name him John, but she knows she's not ready to take care of a baby herself. She hates the idea of having a child and then giving it up for adoption, though. So she's leaning toward having an abortion at this point.

Here's one way a state could make it harder for Jane to have an abortion: it could say minors aren't allowed to have abortions unless they have permission from their parents. Just over half the states in this country have laws requiring a minor to get consent from at least one of her parents before she can have an abortion. If the state where Jane lives has a law like this, that could make it harder for her to get an abortion in two ways. First, Jane might be afraid to ask her parents for permission. Second, even if she does ask them, she might have trouble convincing them to say yes. So laws like this probably prevent a number of teenage girls from having abortions. In addition, a number of states that don't require parental consent still require parental notification. That's not as big a deal but it probably prevents some young women from having abortions, too. They'd rather carry their pregnancy to term than have their parents find out they'd had an abortion. Most states with these kinds of requirements also have an option where a minor who wants an abortion can get permission from a judge instead. But a lot of pregnant teenagers would probably be pretty scared of that prospect, too. So overall, parental consent and notification laws might be a pretty effective way of reducing the number of abortions among minors without actually banning it.

These laws can also seem pretty reasonable. As defenders of parental consent requirements for abortion often point out, there are all sorts of things minors can't do without permission from their parents. In many states, for example, Jane wouldn't be allowed to get a tattoo without written permission from her parents. The same goes for body piercing. But having an abortion is clearly a bigger deal than getting a little bird tattooed on your shoulder or getting your nose pierced. So if a minor needs parental permission to get the tattoo or the piercing, it can seem pretty reasonable to say Jane should need parental permission to get an abortion, too. But is it? Let's see what McFall and Shimp might have to say about the matter.

So suppose David Shimp had just turned seventeen when his cousin was diagnosed with aplastic anemia. At first he thought he'd be happy to help out, but after the initial tests showed he was a promising candidate, he realized he wasn't willing to go through with the procedure and told his cousin his final answer was no. Shimp's mom was the sister of Robert McFall's father, and she told her son in no uncertain terms she wasn't going to take no for an answer. So when McFall took Shimp to court, his lawyer said this: "Your Honor, you have to force Mr. Shimp to let my client use his bone marrow because Mr. Shimp is a minor and his mother says she wants him to let my client use it." Do you think it would be okay for the state to force young Shimp to let McFall use his bone marrow in this version of the story?

I doubt it. If you agree with Judge Flaherty's decision in the real case of *McFall v. Shimp*, you agree McFall didn't have the right to use Shimp's bone marrow in that case. And if you agree McFall didn't have the right to use Shimp's bone marrow in that case, it's hard to see how you could think he would have the right to use it in this case. If McFall had no right to use Shimp's bone marrow in the original case, why would McFall suddenly have this right simply because Shimp was a minor whose mom wanted him to give the bone marrow to McFall?

Here's another way to look at it. Do you think Shimp's mom should have the legal right to force Shimp to give McFall the bone marrow in this version of the story? When I ask if you think Shimp's mom should have this right, I'm not asking if you think she should have the right to say something like "if you don't give your cousin the bone marrow, I'm grounding you for two weeks." I'm asking if you think she should have the right to invoke the power of the state to force her son to give McFall the bone marrow. I find it hard to believe you'd think this. But if the law says Shimp has to give McFall the bone marrow unless Shimp's mom gives him permission not to give McFall the bone marrow, the law effectively gives Shimp's mom the legal right to force Shimp to give McFall the bone marrow. Without his mom's permission, it will be the power of the state, not the threat of being grounded for a few weeks, that will force Shimp to comply. So if you agree Shimp's mom shouldn't have the legal right to force her son to give McFall the bone marrow, you should agree the law shouldn't say Shimp needs his mom's permission to refuse to give McFall the bone marrow.

And if that's what you think about this version of the story of McFall and Shimp, you should think the same thing about the case of Jane and John. If John wouldn't have the right to use Jane's uterus if Jane was 18 years old, why would John suddenly have this right simply because Jane is 17 and her mom wants her to let John use her uterus? And if you're tempted to think that when Jane's a minor, her mom has the right to control how

Jane uses her uterus, ask yourself if you think her mom should have the right to force Jane to get pregnant in the first place. I really doubt you'll think this, and so I really doubt you'll think that when Jane's a minor, her mom has the right to exercise that kind of control over her body. So at least upon reflection, I'm confident you'll agree that if John wouldn't have the right to use Jane's uterus if Jane was 18, he wouldn't have the right to use it just because Jane's 17 and Jane's mom wants her to let John use it. And if the law says Jane has to carry her pregnancy to term unless her mom gives her permission not to, the law effectively gives Jane's mom the legal right to force Jane to carry her pregnancy to term. If Shimp's mom shouldn't have the legal right to force Shimp to let McFall use his bone marrow, then Jane's mom shouldn't have the legal right to force Jane to let John use her uterus. And since this is true even though McFall is a person with a right to life, it's true even if John is a person with a right to life.

While laws requiring minors to get permission from their parents before they can have an abortion might initially seem pretty reasonable, then, I think this version of the story of McFall and Shimp will help you see that they aren't. But what about laws requiring parental consent in other cases, like when a minor wants to get a tattoo or a body piercing? Since having an abortion seems like a bigger deal than getting a tattoo or a piercing, does opposing parental consent laws in the case of abortion mean you also have to oppose parental consent laws in these other cases? No, it doesn't. It doesn't mean this because there's an important difference between abortion and these other cases. In fact, it's the same difference that turned out to explain why opposing mandatory waiting periods in the case of abortion doesn't commit you to opposing mandatory waiting periods in the case of marriage, divorce, and adoption.

When the state forces Shimp to let McFall use his bone marrow because Shimp's mom hasn't given him permission to refuse to let McFall use it, the state forces Shimp to let someone use his body who has no right to use it. It's wrong for the state to force a person to let someone use their body who has no right to use it. This makes it wrong for the state to impose a parental consent requirement on Shimp. If the state forces Jane to carry her pregnancy to term because her mom hasn't given her permission to refuse to let John use her uterus, the state forces Jane to let someone use her body who has no right to use it. So the reason to think it's wrong to require Shimp to get parental consent is also a reason to think it's wrong to require Jane to get parental consent.

But if the state forces a minor to deal with not getting a tattoo or body piercing until they turn 18 because the minor doesn't have parental consent to get the tattoo or piercing, the state doesn't force the minor to let someone do something with their body that they have no right to do. So the reason for thinking it's wrong to require Shimp to get parental consent if he doesn't want to let McFall use his bone marrow and wrong to require Jane to get parental consent if she doesn't want to let John use her uterus is not a reason to think it's wrong to require minors to get parental consent if they want to get a tattoo or a body piercing. Defenders of parental consent requirements in the case of abortion often say if you accept parental consent requirements in the case of tattoos and body piercings, you should accept them in the case of abortion, too. But this version of the story of McFall and Shimp can help us see why this is a mistake. There's a good reason to oppose parental consent requirements in the case of abortion that's perfectly consistent with accepting parental consent requirements in these other cases.

So much for parental consent requirements. What about parental notification requirements? A number of states that don't require parental consent still require parental notification before a minor can have an abortion. If Jane lives in one of these states, she won't need her parent's permission to have an abortion, but the doctor will only be allowed to perform the abortion after they tell at least one of her parents that they're going to do so. Depending on which of these states Jane lives in, they'll either have to tell the parent 24 hours before the abortion can be performed or 48 hours before it can be performed. So part of what these states are doing by imposing parental notification requirements is imposing a mandatory waiting period on minors.

I already explained why I think you should oppose mandatory waiting periods as a general matter in chapter 24, and I don't see why that part of the picture should look any different in the case of minors. If the state forces someone to wait 24 or 48 hours before having an abortion, it forces them to spend 24 or 48 hours letting someone use their body who has no right to use it. It seems just as wrong for a state to do this to a 17-year-old as it would be to do it to an 18-year-old. This means every state that has a parental notification requirement is doing something wrong.

But even though parental notification requirements and mandatory waiting periods go hand in hand this way in practice, there's no reason they can't be pulled apart in principle. A state could require that a minor's parent be notified if she has an abortion without requiring parental consent and without imposing a waiting period. It could do this by saying the parent must be notified immediately after the abortion has taken place. If we want to know if there's anything wrong with parental notification requirements themselves, as opposed to whether there's anything wrong with using parental notification requirements to impose mandatory waiting periods, we should ask what we'd say about a law like this. Would there be anything wrong with it? Let's again ask what McFall and Shimp might have to say about this.

So go back to the version of the story where Shimp had just turned 17 when his cousin was diagnosed with aplastic anemia. But this time, let's say Shimp's mom doesn't know her brother's son is sick and doesn't know he'll die if her son doesn't give him some of his bone marrow. Shimp tells the doctor he doesn't want to let McFall have the bone marrow and the doctor says that's fine. But the doctor also says he can only agree to this if he tells Shimp's mom about it. Shimp explains that he really doesn't want his mom to find out what he's done because he knows she'll be really mad at him. Sorry, the doctor says, nothing I can do about it. State law. If you don't want your mom to find out you refused to let McFall have the bone marrow, then don't refuse to let him have it. You can let him have the bone marrow or I can tell your mom you refused to let him have it. Those are your only options.

What do you think about this version of the story? Part of me thinks you'll object to the law in this case, too—maybe even object to it pretty strongly. If Shimp shouldn't have to get his mom's permission to refuse to give McFall the bone marrow, you might well ask, why should he have to let his mom know about it at all? It's hard to see what the point of the requirement would be if it isn't there just to scare Shimp into letting McFall have the bone marrow. And you'll probably agree it's wrong for the state to try to scare people into donating bone marrow. But part of me thinks you might be okay with the law in this case even if you agree Shimp shouldn't need his mom's permission to say no to giving McFall the bone marrow. You might just think it's the kind of thing a parent has a right to know, even if they don't have a right to do anything about it.

I'm not really sure what you'll think about this case, so I'll simply say this: if you think it would be wrong for the state to impose this restriction on Shimp, you should think it would be wrong to impose it on Jane. If you don't think it would be wrong for the state to impose this restriction on Shimp, there might still be some other reason to think it would be wrong to impose it on Jane, but there might not be. So a parental notification requirement might be okay as long as it's not used as a way of imposing a mandatory waiting period. But regardless of whether you end up thinking parental notification requirements for abortion are okay all by themselves, you should still agree that the way states currently impose them is wrong. That's because the way states currently impose them is by using them to impose mandatory waiting periods for abortion and because it's wrong to impose mandatory waiting periods for abortion for the reasons I gave in chapter 24. And regardless of what you think about parental notification requirements, you should also agree that it's wrong for states to impose parental consent requirements as long as you agree that young Shimp shouldn't need his mom's permission to refuse to let McFall have some of his bone marrow. And since this is what you should think even though McFall was a person with a right to life, this is what you should think even if you think every fetus is a person with a right to life.

# 28

## Other Restrictions

There are a lot more things states can do to make it harder for women to get abortions. It seems like someone comes up with a new one every day. I can't discuss them all here. But that shouldn't be a problem. At this point, you probably get the idea: think about McFall and Shimp.

Suppose a state says women can only have an abortion if it's done in a room of a certain size, for example, or in a building with hallways of a certain width. Eleven states currently have laws that impose the first requirement and ten currently have laws that impose the second one. If you're wondering what you should think about these kinds of laws, you can again turn for guidance to McFall and Shimp. Suppose Shimp tells the doctor he wants to be disconnected from the bone marrow transferring machine and the doctor says something like this: "Personally, I'd be happy to disconnect you from the machine right away, but the state says I can't do that in a building like this because the hallways are too narrow. If you want to get disconnected from the machine, you'll have to get yourself and Mr. McFall here over to the nearest clinic with wider hallways. There's one about 300 miles from here. I think it's open on Mondays and Thursdays."

My guess is you'll find this response unacceptable. If you agree that McFall doesn't have the right to use Shimp's bone marrow, you'll agree that he doesn't have this right regardless of how wide or narrow the hallways are in the building he's in. And if that's what you think about this version of the story of McFall and Shimp, that's what you should think about this kind of attempt to prevent women from having abortions. If it's wrong for the state to force Shimp to let McFall use some of his bone marrow, then it's wrong for the state to force Shimp to spend time letting McFall use his bone marrow by making it harder for him to find a place that will disconnect him from the bone marrow transferring machine. The same goes for pregnant women. If it's wrong for the state to force Alice to let Al use her uterus, then it's wrong for the state to force Alice to spend time letting Al use her uterus by making it harder for Alice to find a place that will provide her with an abortion. And since this is true in the case of McFall and Shimp even though McFall is a person with a right to life, it's true in the case of Alice and Al even if Al is a person with a right to life.

If there are other kinds of abortion restrictions you're interested in, I suggest you evaluate them in the same way. If you're curious about what other kinds of abortion restrictions states have come up with, you might do a little web surfing and then ask what you'd say about comparable attempts to make it harder for Shimp to prevent McFall from continuing to use his bone marrow. My guess is this will lead you to conclude that many current restrictions on abortion, maybe even most, should be abolished. Here's why. On the face of it, at least, there are good arguments in favor of abortion restrictions that impose mandatory waiting periods or require parental consent. The arguments point out that many states impose similar restrictions on other activities, that most people seem to find these restrictions acceptable in those cases, and that abortion seems to be at least as big a deal as those other activities. So, the arguments conclude, if we accept these kinds of restrictions in these other cases, we should accept them in the case of abortion, too.

But many other current restrictions on abortion, perhaps even most, don't have this kind of initial argument in their favor. In many cases, if not most, it's clear that the only rationale for the restriction is to try to force more abortion clinics to close, to try to prevent more people from being allowed to perform abortions, to make abortions more expensive, or in some other way to make it harder for women to have the abortions they have a legal right to have. If I'm right that the case of McFall and Shimp helps us see that even mandatory waiting periods and parental consent requirements are unjustified, despite the initially plausible arguments that can be offered in their defense, it seems all the more unlikely that these other restrictions would turn out to be justified when they don't even have this kind of initial rationale. Suppose a state imposed a restriction that had no other purpose but to make it harder for Shimp to find a place that would disconnect him from the bone marrow transferring machine. I'm pretty sure you'd find that unacceptable regardless of the details. So while I can't take the time here to go one by one through all the abortion restrictions that are currently in place in at least some states, I can say there's a good reason to think you'll find many, maybe even most, unacceptable, if you think about them through the lens of McFall and Shimp.

Having said this, I should add that I'm not saying you'll conclude that all restrictions on abortion are unacceptable. You may well end up thinking there are some cases where there's a good enough reason for the state to do something even though doing it will make things a bit harder for Shimp. As I mentioned in chapter 25, for example, you might well agree that it would be okay to say Shimp can't be disconnected from the bone marrow transferring machine until he's been told how much longer McFall would need to use his bone marrow. That might strike you as an extremely mild imposition on Shimp and one that could be justified by the fact that the information might make a difference to him. If that's what you think about that case, you should be okay with a law that says Alice can't have an abortion until she's first been told how far along her pregnancy is. Of course, maybe that's not what you'll think about that case. Or maybe you'll come up with a few other restrictions you think can be justified in the same way. Maybe even more than a few. I won't hazard a guess about the specifics, but I suspect your responses will still converge around the same general conclusion: that many and perhaps most current restrictions on Alice's right to stop letting Al use her body would be morally unacceptable if they were restrictions on Shimp's right to stop letting McFall use his body. And if I'm right about that, then assuming for the sake of the argument that you haven't found a successful objection to what I said in the first two parts of this book, you should conclude not only that abortion should be legal but also that it should be much less restricted than it currently is even if every fetus is a person with a right to life.

# 29

# Summary and Conclusion

There's a lot more to be said. There are objections I haven't considered here, rebuttals that might be offered to my responses to the objections I did consider, rejoinders I could offer to those rebuttals, and so on. But at this point, it's time to start wrapping things up. So let me conclude by offering a summary of what I've said here and a few comments about what I haven't said. I began part I of this book, in chapter 1, by presenting you with the facts involved in the case of *McFall v. Shimp*. McFall needed Shimp's bone marrow, Shimp refused to provide it, McFall sued Shimp, and the judge sided with Shimp. And I said I was going to assume you agree with the judge that it would be wrong for the state to force Shimp to let McFall use some of his bone marrow. In chapter 2, I then drew a lesson from the case I said you'd have to accept if you did agree with the judge about this: the fact that someone is a person with a right to life doesn't mean they have the right to use another person's body even if they need to use that person's body in order to go on living. And I began to apply this lesson to the problem of abortion, starting with the case of Alice. Alice was raped and found herself pregnant with Al. Defenders of the pro-life position claim the human fetus is a person with a right to life, and I went ahead and assumed for the sake of the argument that they're right about that. They then go on to say that because the fetus has a right to life, abortion is murder and should therefore be illegal. I tried to convince you that the lesson of *McFall v. Shimp* shows this is a mistake. The fact that Robert McFall had a right to life didn't mean he had a right to use another person's body to preserve his life. And if that's true in the case of McFall and Shimp, it must be true in the case of Al and Alice, too. Either having a right to life is enough to give you the right to use another person's body when you need to use it or it isn't. So even if Al has a right to life, that doesn't give him the right to use Alice's body even if he needs to use it to go on living. And if Al has no right to use Alice's body to go on living, then the state has no right to force Alice to let Al use her body to go on living and so has no right to prevent her from having an abortion.

After trying to convince you in chapter 2 that it should be legal for Alice to have an abortion, and after making a few comments about the way I was trying to convince you of this in chapters 3 and 4, I tried to apply the lesson of *McFall v. Shimp* to some other cases. There was Barbara in chapter 5, who got pregnant because her birth control didn't work, and Carol in chapter 6, who got pregnant because she didn't bother using birth control in the first place. There was Dorothy in chapter 7, who was pregnant with a boy but really wanted a girl, and Elaine in chapter 8, who didn't want to carry her pregnancy to term after learning her child would have Down syndrome. In each of these cases I tried to use a variation on the original story of McFall and Shimp to convince you it should be legal for these women to have abortions, too.

In the case of Francine, though, whose pregnancy had already reached the point of viability when I introduced her in chapter 9, I explained why the lesson of *McFall v. Shimp* does not show that it should be legal for her to have an abortion. The same goes for Gloria killing her 3-month-old daughter Gabriella in chapter 10. And in chapter 11, I talked about Heather, who was pregnant with Heath when she was shot and killed by an armed robber. Feticide laws say the gunman can be charged with two counts of homicide in a case like this, and people who are pro-life sometimes say this is hypocritical: how come it's murder if the gunman kills Heath but not if Heather has an abortion? I used another angle on the story of McFall and Shimp to try to show there's really no double standard here. The claim that Shimp should have the right not to let McFall use his bone marrow if he doesn't want to let him use his bone marrow doesn't imply that someone else should have the right to prevent McFall from using Shimp's bone marrow if Shimp decides to let him use it. In the same way, the claim that Heather should have the right not to let Heath use her uterus if she doesn't want to let him use her uterus doesn't imply that someone else should have the right to prevent Heath from using her uterus if Heather decides she does want to let him use it. That concluded the first part of this book.

The overall result of part I, then, was this: if you agree that it would be wrong for the state to force Shimp to let McFall use some of his bone marrow in the various versions of the story I discussed then you should agree that abortion should be legal at least up to the point of viability, no matter how the woman got pregnant and no matter why she doesn't want to remain pregnant, but this doesn't mean you have to agree that abortion should be legal past the point of viability, or that you should think killing children after they've been born should be legal, or deny that killing the fetus of a woman who wants to carry her pregnancy to term should be considered a form of homicide. And since Robert McFall was a person with a right to life, you should think all this even if you think every fetus is a person with a right to life.

I then went on in part II to consider a variety of objections you might have to my argument. Most of these objections arise because there are differences between Shimp's situation and the situation of a pregnant woman. The claim that the fetus has a right to life can't be enough to show that it has a right to continue using the pregnant woman's body. If that was enough to give the fetus the right to use the pregnant woman's body, then the fact that McFall had a right to life and needed to use Shimp's body would have been enough to give McFall the right to use Shimp's body. And it wasn't enough to give McFall that right. But the fetus might still have the right to use the pregnant woman's body even though McFall didn't have the right to use Shimp's body because of some other fact about the woman's situation, a fact that makes her situation different from Shimp's situation. In chapters 12 through 19, I considered a variety of differences a critic of my argument might point to and I tried to show in each case that they don't really undermine my argument. In chapter 20, I considered a few more differences that, if anything, make my argument even stronger. In chapter 21, I considered and responded to two other kinds of objection and that concluded my attempt to anticipate objections you might have and to respond to them.

Finally, in part III, I turned to the question of whether it would be okay for a state to try to reduce the number of abortions that take place by restricting it in various ways without actually banning it. Continuing to assume that every fetus is a person with a right to life, and continuing to turn to different versions of the story of McFall and Shimp for help, I tried to convince you that if my argument in the first two parts of the book was successful, then not only should abortion be legal but many and perhaps most current restrictions on abortion should be abolished.

It would be nice to have a short and snappy slogan to capture all this with, but I haven't been able to come up with one. So I'll have to settle for the following instead. If you agree that it would be wrong for the state to force a person like David Shimp to let someone use some of his bone marrow, you should also agree that it would be wrong for the state to force a pregnant woman to let someone use her uterus. If you agree that many current restrictions on abortion, perhaps even most, would be unacceptable if they were imposed on people like Shimp who don't want to let someone use their bone marrow, you should also agree that many current restrictions on abortion, perhaps even most, are unacceptable when they are imposed on pregnant women who don't want to let someone use their uterus. If you think it would be wrong for the state to treat someone like Shimp in these ways even though Robert McFall was a person with a right to life, you should also think it is wrong for the state to treat pregnant women in these ways even if you think every fetus is a person with a right to life. And if you think it would be wrong for the state to treat Shimp in these ways even if you think it was immoral for Shimp to refuse to let McFall use his bone marrow, you should also think it is wrong for the state to treat pregnant women in these ways even if you think it is immoral for a pregnant woman to refuse to let a fetus use her uterus. If you think what I'm guessing you'll think about the case of McFall and Shimp, that is, you should conclude that abortion should be legal and much less restricted than it currently is even if you think abortion is immoral and even if you think every fetus is a person with a right to life. That's what I've said in this book.

It may also be worth stressing a few things I haven't said in this book. First, I haven't said the right to control your body is absolute. The lesson of *McFall v. Shimp* is not that the state should let you do anything you want with your body. It isn't even that it's always wrong for the state to force you to do something with your body or always wrong for it to forcibly do something to your body. The lesson is simply that it would be wrong for the state to force you to let another person use your body even if they need to use it. Or, at least, that it's wrong for the state to do this in cases where the burden this would impose on you would be at least as great as the burden involved in having some of your bone marrow extracted. So you don't have to hold some radical or absolutist view about bodily autonomy in order to accept my defense of abortion rights. You just have to agree that it would have been wrong for the state to force Shimp to let McFall have some of his bone marrow.

Second, I haven't said the differences between Shimp and a pregnant woman are morally irrelevant. The differences I talked about in part II may turn out to make a difference to your moral judgments. You might end up thinking that having an abortion is morally worse than what Shimp did, that what Shimp did is morally worse than having an abortion, or that the two are morally on a par. It doesn't matter. What matters is that the differences between Shimp and a pregnant woman aren't relevant to the question of whether it would be okay for the state to force them to let another person use their body. All I tried to show in part II is that the differences between the two cases aren't relevant in that respect. So long as you agree that it would be wrong for the state to force Shimp to let McFall use his bone marrow in the versions of the story that made Shimp more like a pregnant woman in various ways, it doesn't matter if the changes to the story affect your moral judgment about Shimp. If after taking the differences into account you still think it would be wrong for the state to force Shimp to let McFall use his bone marrow, then you should still think it would be wrong for the state to force the woman to let the fetus use her uterus regardless of whether you think it would be immoral for her to refuse to let the fetus use her uterus.

Finally, I haven't said you should find the argument of this book convincing if you disagree with Judge Flaherty's decision. I started out by assuming you agree that it would be wrong for the state to force Shimp to let McFall use his bone marrow. If you don't accept that assumption, you don't have any reason to accept my argument. On the assumption that you did agree with the judge's decision when you started reading this book, though, it's worth noting that I've also been making a second assumption: I've been assuming if I could convince you that the state's forcing Shimp to let McFall use his bone marrow is like the state's forcing a pregnant woman to let the fetus use her uterus, you'd conclude that it would be wrong for the state to force the woman to let the fetus use her uterus. And while this second assumption seems reasonable, I admit I might be wrong. If you started out thinking abortion should be illegal and that the judge was right, and if you came to agree with me that the two cases should stand or fall together, you might conclude that the judge was wrong about McFall and Shimp rather than that you were wrong about abortion. Instead of concluding that it would be wrong for the state to force someone to let another person use their body in both cases, you might conclude that it would be okay for the state to do this in either case.

Leading you to this conclusion was obviously not my intention in writing this book. But if that's the conclusion you come away with, I won't try to argue you out of it here. Instead, I'll just ask you to consider how much punishment you think the state should inflict if the law required Shimp to remain connected to the bone marrow transferring machine and his friends helped to disconnect him. It's hard to believe you'll think they should get anything more than a modest fine. Vermont, for example, is one of the few states that legally requires people to offer "reasonable assistance" to those who are in grave danger, and the maximum penalty for violating the law is a $100 fine. Even if you think donating bone marrow to another person is a form of "reasonable assistance" that should be legally required, this suggests the penalties for refusing to donate it should be quite mild. And if that's right, then even if you conclude that laws requiring bone marrow donation and laws requiring women to carry their pregnancies to term should stand together rather than fall together, you should conclude that while abortion should be illegal, the penalties for those who break the law should be quite modest. Like littering, abortion should technically be illegal, but anyone who wants to do it can do it, as long as they're willing to pay a modest fine if they're caught. It's probably not a position that would make either side in the debate over abortion particularly happy, but if you find no fault with my argument and are unwilling to accept its conclusion, that may be the best you can do. In any event, there are obviously many more things that I haven't said in this book, but I won't say anything more about any of them here. I hope it's clear by now what I've said here and what I haven't.

If you've been convinced by what I have said here, that's great. I hope you'll feel motivated to do something about it. The current threat to abortion rights is real and there's a lot that can be done. If you aren't convinced, well, it certainly won't be the first time. I've been thinking on and off about the kind of argument I've tried to extract from the case of *McFall v. Shimp* here for over twenty-five years. I've had conversations with hundreds of people about it over that time, written a few articles, participated in several debates, published one previous book, and corresponded with plenty of readers and critics who contacted me online. It's hard to say how many people end up finding my view convincing and how many don't, but I'd guess my batting average is pretty low. So, like I said, if you're not convinced by what I've said here, you won't be the first.

Still, even if you haven't been convinced to accept the position I've tried to defend here, I hope you've at least been convinced of a few things. If you think abortion should be legal but for reasons other than mine, I hope you've at least been convinced that the position I've taken here can serve as a worthy complement to your position, rather than as a distracting rival. If you think abortion should be legal because you don't think the fetus is a person with a right to life, for example, I hope you'll consider that your position might be strengthened by appealing to mine as a kind of backup. If you think abortion should be legal because of the effect it would have on gender equality if women were forced to carry their unplanned pregnancies to term, I hope you'll consider that your position might be strengthened by incorporating mine into it in the way I briefly suggested in chapter 21.

But perhaps more importantly, if you haven't been convinced by what I've said here and you think abortion should be illegal, I hope you'll at least be convinced that there's more to the pro-choice position than you may have realized. And if you're going to continue to maintain that abortion should be illegal, I hope you'll at least be convinced that you'll have to say more than just that the fetus has a right to life if you want to justify your position. If nothing else, I hope you've been convinced that the mere fact that the fetus is a person with a right to life, assuming it is a fact, can't be enough by itself to give the fetus a right to use the pregnant woman's body even if the fetus needs to use that body to go on living. If just having a right to life were enough to give a person the right to use another person's body when they needed it, after all, then Robert McFall would have had the right to use David Shimp's bone marrow. And I doubt you think he did. This doesn't have to mean there isn't some other reason to think the fetus has a right to use the pregnant woman's body. But it does mean you have to identify that other reason pretty clearly and pretty carefully if you're going to try to justify the claim that the power of the state should be used to force women to carry their pregnancies to term.

And I hope you've at least been convinced by engaging with this book that there's room for reasonable, respectful, and constructive dialogue between people who are pro-life and people who are pro-choice. It isn't always easy to be convinced of this when you look at the way the debate about abortion is often carried out in this country. But I think it's true. I'm a philosopher, and philosophers often write as if what we're offering is meant to be the last word on the subject at hand. Admitting doubts or expressing reservations can almost be seen as bad form. But if you're someone who thinks abortion should be illegal and yet you've taken the time to read this book despite our disagreement, I want to conclude by offering you my gratitude, not by insisting that I must be right and you must be wrong. So I'll simply end by saying I don't pretend to be having the last word here. And if you're still inclined to think abortion should be illegal, I hope you'll take seriously the words I've offered here, last word or not, before deciding what your own last word on the subject should be.

# Postscript

The argument I offered in this book is a variation on an argument first put forward by Judith Jarvis Thomson in her classic article "A Defense of Abortion." The fictional version of McFall and Shimp that I introduced in chapter 3 is based on the famous example involving an unconscious violinist that she appeals to in that work. Thomson's article was originally published in *Philosophy and Public Affairs* in 1971 and has since been reprinted in numerous anthologies. If you're interested in thinking more about the merits of the kind of argument I've offered here, Thomson's article is the place to start.

A little over thirty years after Thomson's article first appeared, I published a book that was also called *A Defense of Abortion* (Cambridge University Press, 2003). That book, like Thomson's article, focused on the question of whether abortion is morally permissible rather than on the question of whether abortion should be legal. But my discussion of Thomson's argument in chapter 4 of that book may be useful if you want to think more about the argument in either context. The chapter considers a variety of objections in more detail than I have been able to go into here and discusses a variety of published responses to Thomson's original argument that you might also want to look at. Among the books that have appeared since mine was published and that raise important objections to the kind of argument I've defended here, you might want to look at Francis J. Beckwith's *Defending Life* (Cambridge University Press, 2007) and Christopher Kaczor's *The Ethics of Abortion* (Routledge, 2011) among others.

Keeping up with the abortion literature is hard. Keeping up with abortion law is even harder. Hardly a day seems to go by without some new restriction being introduced or enacted or struck down. The specific examples I've referred to here should be current as of December 2017, but by the time this book is in print, things may already have changed. If you're interested in any of the details, there are a variety of reliable online sources that are frequently updated.

As for the real-life story of McFall and Shimp, an article published in the *Michigan Daily* on Friday, August 11, 1978, reports that shortly before his death, McFall forgave his cousin for refusing to donate the bone marrow he needed and asked his family to forgive him, too. His sister, Beverly Hope, is even quoted as saying of Shimp that "[w]e know he's an individual and has his own right to a decision." You can find the article online if you want to learn a little more about the story, and you can find the full text of Judge Flaherty's decision online, too.

Finally, I would like to thank the University of Colorado for providing me with a paid sabbatical during the fall 2016 semester and the College of Arts and Sciences for granting me a College Scholar Award for the spring 2017 semester. Most of the work on this book was done during that period and I would not have been able to complete it without this assistance. I wouldn't have been able to work on this book in the first place were it not for the thoughtful feedback I've received over the years from people too numerous to list here: friends, colleagues, students, teachers, critics, audience members, writers, scholars, activists, and family members. I'm grateful to everyone whose writings, questions, or comments have helped me to better understand the nature and limits of the kind of argument I've offered in this book.

# Index

abortion counseling, 157, 160–61, 169–79
abortion pill, 109–10, 112–13, 116
abortion waiting periods, 157–68, 190, 191–92, 193–94, 196–97
Alabama, 164
Arizona, 37–38, 182
Arkansas, 164

Beckwith, Francis J., 209–10
Blackmun, Harry, ix
burdens of pregnancy, 128–32

California, 52–53
child support laws, 84–86
Christian Scientists, 154
consent, 60–67
contraceptive failure cases, 21–27, 60–67, 71–83, 84–86, 149, 200

dilation and curettage, 108–9, 110–12, 114–15, 116–18

Down syndrome cases, 41–42, 125–26, 149–50, 200

fetal abnormalities, see Down syndrome cases
fetal homicide ("feticide") laws, 52–56, 200–1
fetal pain, 114, 175–76, 179
Flaherty, John P., Jr., 3, 5, 11, 131, 210
Florida, 184

gender equality, 132–34, 206–7
God, 100–1, 105–6

health insurance restrictions, 144–49, 158–60, 161
Hyde Amendment, 151–56
Hyde, Henry, 151
hypothetical versus actual cases, 18–19
hysterotomy, 109–12, 116–19

Indiana, 41–42, 184
infanticide, 49–51, 200–1

intending versus foreseeing, 121–25
Iowa, 164

Jehovah's Witnesses, 154

Kaczor, Christopher, 209–10
Kansas, 37–38
killing versus letting die, 107–19

Louisiana, 41–42, 171–72, 182

Maryland, 163–64
McFall, Robert, 3, 5, 210
*McFall v. Shimp*, 3, 5, 9
Medicaid, 151–56
Michigan, 172–73
Missouri, 144–45, 172–73

natural functions, 100–5
natural selection, 100–1, 102, 105–6
New Hampshire, 163–64
North Carolina, 37–38, 184
North Dakota, 37–38, 41–42

Ohio, 172–73, 184
Oklahoma, 37–38

parental consent requirements, 187–91, 193–94, 196–97
parental notification requirements, 187, 191–93

parental obligations, 88–95, 96–98
Pennsylvania, 37–38
punishment for abortion, 205–6

rape cases, 7, 9–12, 13, 88–95, 96–98, 199–200
responsibility, 69–83
*Roe v. Wade*, ix, x

sex selection cases, 37–39, 125–26, 149–50, 200
sex without contraception cases, 31–34, 149, 200
Shimp, David, 3, 5, 210
South Carolina, 163–64
South Dakota, 37–38, 157
starting versus continuing to provide bodily support, 13–16

Texas, 171–72
Thomson, Judith Jarvis, ix, x, 209

ultrasound, 157, 160–61, 181–86
Unborn Victims of Violence Act (2004), 52–53

Vermont, 205
viability, 45–48, 109–10, 113, 119–20, 200–1
Virginia, 182

Washington, 164
Wisconsin, 171–72